Conversion and Christian Character

Conversion and Christian Character

SAMUEL SOUTHARD

BROADMAN PRESS • Nashville, Tennessee

DEWEY DECIMAL CLASSIFICATION: 248

Library of Congress catalog card number: 65–15600

Printed in the United States of America

12. F65 KSP

To

Frances, Pamela, and Melanie

Contents

Contents

1

The Challenge of Conversion

Salvation cannot be separated from discipleship. No man can call Jesus Lord unless he does the things that Christ commands (cf. Luke 6:46). To be a new creation in Christ Jesus is to have a new point of view, which guides one's growth in grace. Such is the theme of this book.

The focus will be on the new point of view of a converted man. Jonathan Edwards called this "the new sense" of religion that comes to those who accept God's call. As the apostle Paul writes in 2 Corinthians 5, one who is in Christ has a different point of view because he is a new creation.

The organization of inner attitudes in the spirit of Christ has many names. Psychologically, it can be called the process of self-identification; morally, it is the development of character; theologically, it is strengthening of the inner man. These three points of view bring together a man's relationship to himself, to others, and to God.

Jesus described Christian character in terms of the heart. In the good man the center of the self is a good treasure that bears good fruit (cf. Luke 6:43–45). To Paul, the man who leads a life worthy of his calling is one in whom the Holy Spirit dwells. He who is filled with the fulness of Christ will grow up into mature knowledge and stature (cf. Eph. 3:14 to

4:16). We are not disciples unless we are following Jesus'
example.

Turning Toward Discipleship

The character of a Christian depends upon his Christlike-
ness. This remolding of personality begins in conversion,
which is the turning of a man's mind and heart and life in the
direction of God as revealed through Christ Jesus. For the
Christian, conversion is the first stage in the pilgrimage initi-
ated by God by which life is transformed. There is a shift in
the habitual center of being, a movement of one's life force
into a new channel. In biblical language, it is a new creation
(cf. 2 Cor. 5:17); the indwelling of Christ in the heart by faith
(cf. Eph. 3:17); a new birth (cf. John 3:3); redemption from
all iniquity (cf. Titus 2:14); passing out of death into life
(cf. John 5:24).

Conversion is the beginning of a new point of view concerning the past, the present, and the future. When a Christian
looks to the past he acknowledges the gracious acts of God in
history for the redemption of mankind. He can be grateful for
the stirring of the Holy Spirit in his own life that has brought
him by grace to confess Christ as Saviour and to release the
grip of guilt that binds his soul for past mistakes. Conversion
does not change a man's memory, but it does clarify it. The
power of Christ enables one to observe his "natural face in a
mirror" and compare this with the law of God. The hopeless-
ness of past sins does not cause one to forget what he is really
like (cf. James 1:22–25).

The converted man also may have a new view of the
present. Fellowship with Christ and his people gives a divine
power for a new life today (cf. 1 Thess. 1:5; Rom. 15:13). In
the present time he is renewed (cf. 2 Cor. 4:10–18) or made
alive (cf. Eph. 2:1). There is no mourning for past experiences.
This does not mean that a convert is to be satisfied with

his present existence. Salvation gives one a wider view of the future. There is challenge and hope in Paul's words: "Work out your own salvation with fear and trembling; for God is at work in you" (Phil. 2:12–13). The Christian presses on toward the completion of his redemption (cf. 1 Cor. 15:42–58; Phil. 3:12–16). He does not yet know what God will make of him; it is enough to know that he is being remade in the image of God's Son. In its fullest sense, which we seldom attain, conversion gives us a clean memory of the past, a clear view of our present state, and a challenging life for the future.

The Variety of Conversion Experiences

What does the biblical teaching on conversion mean for us today? First, we can recognize that Jesus called men to him in many different ways. There is only one Lord whom we are to serve, but we come to him through a variety of conversion experiences.

John, Andrew, and Peter came to Jesus out of wonder, admiration, and a sense of life fulfilment (cf. John 1:35–51). The Philippian jailer found salvation in the midst of a great crisis (cf. Acts 16:19–34). The Samaritan woman had a long talk with Jesus and then went away asking, "Can this be the Christ?" (John 4:29).

Theologians who have been active in evangelism have recognized the individual differences in the process of regeneration. E. Y. Mullins wrote:

> While repentence and faith are central and essential in every conversion, there are many varieties in the experience of those who find Christ. The point of emphasis varies with the individual. With some love seems to be the dominating motive. With others it is obedience, with others hope; and in some cases merely the desire to do right is the chief motive.[1]

---

[1] *Talks on Soul-Winning* (Nashville: Sunday School Board, Southern Baptist Convention, 1920), p. 18.

Psychological studies of conversion have also noted these differences. Edwin Starbuck noticed that the revivalistic preaching of his day (1899) produced much storm and stress in adolescence. These were the individuals who most often reported a climactic conversion experience. But E. T. Clark, surveying conversion thirty years later, found less than 7 per cent of converts who reported a definite crisis experience. By this time, the age of commitment to Christ had dropped from sixteen to twelve. As one study by Robert Ferm shows, persons who join the church in childhood tend to have a gradual or extremely mild experience.

Age makes a difference. If the conversion is of an adult who has been an outsider to the church, then the decision may include a strong upsurge of emotion. Mature patterns of life are disrupted in the upsurge of a godly center for the new man.

The personality as well as the way of life will condition a person's response to the Saviour. William James observed that "healthy-minded" men are born only once. They have a sense of union with God from an early age that is not accompanied by deep feelings of remorse or guilt at any time.

On the other hand, there are "sick souls" who writhe under conviction of sin. These are persons who know evil from personal experience. Their world has been stamped with failure and they have known the blackness of melancholy. To them, Christianity means deliverance, a second birth, the unification of a divided self.[2]

From the brief references in the Scriptures, we might think of John, Philip, and Andrew as examples of a quiet call to follow Christ. Other disciples' lives, like Simon Peter, Zacchaeus, or the Philippian jailer, were literally turned about

---

[2] William James was speaking of our awareness of imperfections. Although some Christians may be "healthy-minded," the biblical view places all men under the indictment of sin.

by the Lord. In fact, Jesus used a word with that meaning when he told Peter, "When you have turned again [art converted, KJV], strengthen your brethren" (Luke 22:32).

Theological teaching may lead a person toward a particular type of religious experience. E. T. Clark found that persons who had been raised under a "stern theology" tended more toward a climactic conversion than other converts. At times, people believe that the serious preaching of sin and salvation requires a particular kind of emotional response. Despite the variegated treasure of biblical experiences with Christ, there are some evangelists who teach that *every* convert must have a great feeling of remorse and an open display of emotion before he is truly converted.

A great evangelist like Charles G. Finney condemned this rigid systemization of conversion. In his *Lectures on Revivals of Religion*, he wrote, "Great evils have arisen, and many false hopes have been created by not *discriminating between an awakened and a convicted sinner*," Finney concluded that indiscriminate exhortations to repent had greatly injured revivals.

Dwight L. Moody recognized the individuality of repentance when he wrote in *Great Joy* that God never repeats himself. He does not approach any two people the same way. Mr. Moody taught his soul-winning classes, "If you are going to be successful in winning souls to Christ you need discrimination in finding out people's differences."

Are we to conclude from these statements that there is no definite commitment to be asked of one who accepts Christ as Saviour? No. The protest of theologians, perceptive evangelists, and psychologists is only against the elevation of one method of conversion above all others. There is a danger that the rigid identification of conversion with the techniques of a previous generation will cause many people to reject "revivalism" altogether. This is a Christian tragedy, for there is some truth in those who uphold a cataclysmic experience and some accuracy to the contention that Christian conversion should be gradual and serene. As we have already seen, the age, personality, relation to the church, and theological teaching will condition an individual's response. Why should we try to insist upon our way as the only one? Jesus told Nicodemus quite frankly that the Spirit of God, like the wind, blows where it will.

The essential theological imperative of conversion is commitment and dedication to Christ. Whether a person comes abruptly and explosively or through the quiet culmination of maturing convictions, there must be a time of private and public affirmation of Christ as Saviour and Lord. Each unique pattern of personality must be transformed in the light of one question, "Whom do *you* say that I am?" The answer must always be the same: "The Christ of God" (Luke 9:20), but the *way* in which a man finds that answer will be his own.

The Fruit of the Spirit

A second application of biblical passages on conversion is the imperative to grow in grace. The reformation of a person in Christ must follow the spiritual death of an old self. Exhortations, examples, and criteria for Christian growth are found throughout the New Testament (cf. Acts 11:23; Heb. 3:13–14; Jude 20; 1 Peter 2:5–8; 1 Cor. 15:1–2; 2 Cor. 1:24; Gal. 6:1; Phil. 1:27; 2:1–13; 3:12–16; Eph. 3:14–19; Rom. 8:18–39). The Christian life is continually described as an ongoing struggle: "In all these things we keep on gloriously conquering through Him who loved us" (Rom. 8:37, Williams).

These biblical exhortations are especially needed in churches that have tried to separate Christ as Lord from Christ as Saviour. Some persons are so fascinated by explosive conversion experiences that they ignore the subsequent need to replace the pieces of a shattered life. They forget the warning of Jesus, that a man whose life is cleansed but vacant may take worse spirits than he had before (cf. Luke 11:24–26). Charles Spurgeon gave the same warning in *The Soul-Winner*:

Some of the most glaring sinners known to me were once members of a church; and were, as I believe, led to make a profession by undue pressure, well-meant but ill-judged. . . . It very often happens that the converts that are born in excitement die when the excitement is over. . . . I delight not in the religion which needs or creates a hot head. Give me the godliness which flourishes upon Calvary rather than upon Vesuvius.

These warnings apply to modern Baptist churches. In 1953, C. E. Matthews concluded that "48.4 per cent of the entire membership of Southern Baptist churches is lost to the cause of Christ." [3]

In a study of converts one year after a revival, Professor Liston Mills of Vanderbilt Divinity School classified the new Baptists of "First Church" as follows:

Those who are regular in church attendance and assume some responsibility as a member of a church committee, an officer, or a teacher, 6 per cent.
Those who consider themselves to be members in good standing, attend fairly often or regularly the Sunday school and/or Sunday morning worship service, 42 per cent.
Those who consider themselves to be members of the church but almost never attend any of its services, 50 per cent.
Those who were voted into the church after they walked down the aisle but who never returned to the church, 2 per cent.

Mills and his associates interviewed friends and church people who knew these converts. Many converts had to think for some time before they could suggest the name of a friend

---

[3] *A Church Revival* (Nashville: Broadman Press, 1955), p. 103.

in the church or any friend who might give the pastor an evaluation of their confession of faith and change of life. One boy remarked, "Well I don't think that any of my friends know that I am supposed to be a Christian."

When children joined the church and thereby united a family in Christian faith, they continued to be active in the fellowship. But when no one cared for an isolated child who was converted, he soon stopped growing and often stayed home on Sunday. When a father or mother joined the church and united a family, or when a man was given strong support by friends in the neighborhood or congregation, then the new member was consistent and fruitful. But when conversion was treated with indifference by church members and neighbors and family members, then an adult convert might easily drift away. As one adult, who had been inactive in the church, expressed it: "I don't understand some people who claim to be Christians. Some of them will speak at church, but if they meet you on the street or any place away from the church they act like they don't even know you."

Although there is little visible connection between Christian growth and conversion in many lives, there still are persons who demonstrate the ongoing character of Christian faith. For example, in four rural Baptist churches in Kentucky, adult men in Sunday school classes were asked to describe their conversion. Eighteen out of twenty-six spoke of their experience as a gradual process. Most of them thought about salvation for several years before they made a public profession. They were influenced by their parents, friends, the church, and the Sunday school. These channels of grace led them to the day of decision in late childhood or adolescence. One man said that it was like the unfolding of a flower's petals: "Whether the experience took place in a Sunday school classroom, church service, or at my mother's knee would be impossible to say."

The men also felt that there was a definite sense of spiritual relief and newness of life when they made their profession of faith. As one of the men put it: "It was like a burden lifted off my shoulders and everything took on a new meaning."

The men described changes both in attitude and in conduct. Some of the phrases were: "I am somebody now. I want to bring the same life to others"; "I realized I was on the wrong path and began immediately to improve my conduct"; "I now find that sin is disgusting."

Over the years, the men demonstrated varying degrees of spirituality. For some, there would be a gradual increase of dedication to a plateau where they felt serene in their faith. Others moved from mountaintop to valley and back to mountaintop. If a crisis arose it would be solved through a revival or through the influence of Christian friends. Then there would be a gradual loss of interest until again the need for rededication became evident. Other men moved along an indefinite path, following conversion, until something happened to deepen their faith. One man wrote: "I let my business problems get the best of me. Then I felt empty inside with no hope in sight, but then I felt a new awareness of God, holding out his hand if I would take it. Thus I believe conversion experiences are taking place at all times."

If the reports of these men are typical, we may be assured that growth does take place following conversion, although it may be uneven. Jesus, describing growth in grace in the eighth chapter of Luke, said that there will be some personalities so hard that little or no results can be seen. Or, the soil of the soul may be receptive and growth may be obvious. In other cases the shallowness of the individual will result in a withering away and a necessity of a fresh renewal of faith.

Another application of New Testament teaching is the necessity for judgment of spiritual experience. This teaching has been neglected among Baptists in the past fifty years,

until confession of faith often has been reduced to "yes" and a
few brief answers to questions asked by the pastor at the conclusion of a church service.

As J. L. Dagg, influential Southern Baptist theologian and
president of Mercer University, wrote:

> The churches are not infallible judges, being unable to search
> the heart; but they owe it to the cause of Christ, and to the candi-
> date himself, to exercise the best judgment of which they are
> capable. To receive any one on a mere profession of words, with-
> out an effort to ascertain whether he understands and feels what
> he professes, is unfaithfulness to his interests, and the interests of
> religion.

What is it that we are asked to judge? Certainly not the
inner workings of God's grace, for no man can fathom this.
But we are to examine the fruit of the spirit, which is the sign
among men that a life is regenerate (cf. Gal. 5:16–24). Like a
skilful physician, we are to know the signs of spiritual growth
or decay among those who inquire about salvation. E. Y. Mullins has called this "spiritual diagnosis."

What are some modern characteristics of a conversion
that grows into Christian character?

A well-defined conversion experience.—The person is able
to tell that his life is different. In the case of an explosive
turning about, the evidence may be quite obvious. If the conversion is gradual the individual should be able to state how
his way of looking at things is different from that of persons
who are not allied with Christ.

A full life.—A maturing conversion is a growing experience. Paul wrote the Philippians that those who are mature
will "press on toward the goal for the prize of the upward call
of God in Christ Jesus" (Phil. 3:14). The saved person does
not confine his faith to one narrow channel of life. He is willing
to examine his social and racial attitudes, his business prac-

tices, and his family responsibilities in the light of Christ's pure love.

A consistent morality.—The writer to the Hebrews warned that those who "go on to maturity" will not crucify the Son of God again by holding him up to contempt (cf. Heb. 6:1-8). A dynamic Christian experience enables a man to examine one area of life after another in the spirit of Christ. Lifelong pride, secret habits, ancient and modern prejudices will be transformed. Each part of a man's religious experience should be progressively connected with every other part. A person who has experienced the new birth can see that the judgment and love of God go together. Later we will discuss the relationship of some of these areas of Christian experience.

A maturing convert is a humble learner.—He does not boast about his new knowledge in Christ nor act as though he knows all things. He does not magnify his certainties to condemn all differences. The apostle Paul warned those who were arrogant that "the kingdom of God does not consist in talk but in power" (1 Cor. 4:20).

All these godly characteristics are summarized in 1 John 4:16: "God is love, and he who abides in love abides in God, and God abides in him." A life full of love is a sign of God's purposes fulfilled in us. This is a continual New Testament emphasis, and will be the theme for the final chapter of this book.

By contrast with a loving rebirth there are other "conversions" that do not "grow up in every way into him who is the head, into Christ" (Eph. 4:15). Instead, the unfolding character of the individual is far from Christ. Such conversions often begin with an exaggerated zeal in which the "convert" tries to do everything. This is often followed by an abrupt coolness and lack of interest in the new faith. Today the zealot condemns Christians who do not move heaven and earth because of his enthusiasm. But tomorrow his story is different. He finds great obstacles and blames others for his backsliding. Yet, he is difficult to convict of sin and remains a nominal member of the church.

The "stillborn" convert is preoccupied with the form of religion. He shows little interest in the great principles of faith. He is disturbed by any change in the order of worship, such as reading from a new translation of the Bible or the buying of new hymnals. Everything should be left just as it was when he made a profession of faith five, ten, or twenty years ago.

The "regressive" convert hates everyone who was connected with his former way of life. Blame for former actions is placed on others. His "holier than thou" attitude turns acquaintances against him.

An "abortive conversion" magnifies spiritual pride. Such a convert is still filled with self-love and now has religion as a club to use on anyone who disagrees with his position.

The ungodly convert rushes toward conspicuous martyrdom. His attitude deliberately provokes attack from others. This is his proof that he alone is righteous. In a later chapter we will see how this is distinguished from the prophetic spirit.

The "misguided" convert abandons family responsibilities. A woman may wander about the community, gossiping with anyone who will listen, while her husband and children take care of the house. A husband, whether ordained or unordained, will excuse himself from family responsibilities by saying that he must continually "be about the Lord's work."

These characteristics of unfruitful conversions are the opposite of Christ's spirit. "Not every one who says to me, 'Lord, Lord,' shall enter the kingdom of heaven, but he who does the will of my Father who is in heaven" (Matt. 7:21). To be a disciple is more than saying yes to a minister before a congregation of people; it is also a life of obedience to the will of God.

2
The Christian Conscience

How is a person to know that he is doing the will of God? What is the standard by which a new convert is to judge his spiritual growth? Just what are the ways by which a person receives God's grace?

There are at least three guides to Christian growth: a transformed conscience; study of the Old and New Testaments; and redemptive participation in a Christian fellowship. These channels of grace have one common source—the spirit of Christ. At different ages, and under different circumstances, individuals will find more guidance from one than from another. But each aspect of inspiration reinforces the others. Without all three, guidance is incomplete.

A knowledge of Christ's ministry is necessary to instruct the vague feelings of a convert about right and wrong. The discipline of Christian fellowship is necessary to expand the understanding of a person who only reads the portions of the Bible that agree with his preconceptions.

Let's explore the sources of a godly conscience. The first source is the new perception of self. One begins to see himself, not in light of what he thinks himself to be, but rather in light of what God wants him to be. He is developing a conscience. He affirms his faith. He realizes he is not perfect,

21

that he still makes mistakes, but with God's help he can with Paul press on "toward the mark for the prize of the high calling of god in Christ Jesus." Second, in his earthly ministry Jesus laid down some principles by which the Christian is to live. Each person must seek to apply these principles in whatever situation he may find himself. Third, church and family will influence one's ability to know right from wrong.

A New Perception of Self

At the threshold of man's awareness of God is the conscience. A conscience is so crucial to Christian growth that some people say, "Let your conscience be your guide." After all, it is a voice within insisting that we do certain things.

But conscience by itself does not tell us what is right in the sight of God. Our ideas of right and wrong are gathered from many sources—custom, example of parents, play of children, personal passion, the life and words of godly people, the books we read, and so on.

With so many sources and such differing voices, the conscience of man is not a very reliable guide. To be of value, one's conscience must be shaped by the loving force of a Christian home and community. This inner voice of praise and blame must be redeemed by the Holy Spirit. Our view of right and wrong must be measured by the supreme example of Jesus' life, as it is recorded in the Scriptures.

The development of conscience.—The development of a person's conscience will have much to do with the accuracy or inaccuracy of his perception of God. It takes a long time for one to develop mature sensitivity and understanding.

One of the first tasks of conscience would hardly seem to be religious. The early moral training of a child centers about the functions of his own body. This is all that he can control. The chairman of the Committee on Human Development of the University of Chicago, Dr. Robert Havighurst, lists toilet-training as a basic stamp upon the child's later character.

When we reflect upon this statement, some of the moral significance can be seen. The patient parent, who waits until a child is old enough to know when he is wet, can appeal to the child's dawning awareness of responsibility. An impatient parent wants the child to meet adult demands before the child has physical control of his own needs.

On the basis of patient requirements from parents, a child can learn that social expectations are reasonable. Only that which he can know and perform is required. After he has consistent control, there still may be an occasional problem when he is relaxed in sleep. Then a parent has an opportunity to teach something about forgiveness and understanding, when he recognizes that the child is too young to have "perfect" control.

An impatient parent misses these opportunities for moral teaching and considers the cleanliness and dryness of a child only in terms of the adult's convenience.

The emphasis of a considerate parent is upon the development of a moral task at a time when the child is able to respond. There is praise and there is punishment, but it is a balance between the convenience of the parents and the growing abilities of a boy or girl. Usually at age four or five the child is able to take praise and blame. He then makes the words of his parents his own.

One father observed this as his son was trying to take a nap in the next room. The boy would slip a leg off the bed, but as soon as his foot touched the floor he would say to himself, "Foot, get back up in the bed!" After five minutes of reciting Daddy's words for him, the little one turned over in the bed and went to sleep. This young man had already developed some trust and self-direction in his first four years of life. He had been shown some directions in life by people who are reliable, but they had also taught him self-reliance by encouraging him to stand up by himself, form words, open and close doors, turn a television volume up or down, and get in and out of bed for himself.

It will be some time before the youngster will know how to use praise and punishment appropriately toward himself, but at least the ingredients of morality are now within.

When a child moves from home to school, his conscience expands. If he has learned to identify with his parents as wholesome people, he can now begin to trust and obey teachers and other adults with authority.

He is also confronted with the necessity of co-operating with other children. It is not enough to obey teacher. There are also rules for play and conduct that are worked out by his friends and enemies. So at age seven or eight, the child begins to "play right," whether an adult is watching or not. He has learned that this is the way to have fun with his fellows. He is beginning to use the voice of conscience for himself.

It is at this point that some childish consciences begin to cause trouble. Why? Because the child has been taught *absolute* obedience to any whim of his parents. He thinks that there can be no question of adult rules. Literal obedience is required. So, in a play situation, the child either throws all restraints away and disrupts a game or insists that the rules must be played as he learned them. Even if he keeps quiet, he is very uncomfortable. His "conscience bothers him." In some vague way he is aware that his parents might be displeased because he is not playing a game the way they taught him.

This is the *authoritarian conscience*. It is to be distinguished from the *rational conscience*, in which a child has been encouraged to see when his parents' orders should be absolutely obeyed and when circumstances would modify them. For example, an eight-year-old girl had been playing near the edge of a fish pond and her mother was afraid she would get wet. The mother, busy talking to friends, waved her hand at the daughter and said: "Go over and sit on the park bench until I call you. I don't want you to get dirty before we leave this party." Several minutes later the mother found her daughter some distance from the bench, looking at a flower bed. When the parent became angry, the child replied, "But, Mama, I did not want to stay where you told me to go because the bench had a wet paint sign on it. I was *trying* to keep my dress clean, like you said."

"You are a smart daughter," replied the mother. The child had determined what means were most appropriate to fulfil a legitimate demand, even though she was "literally" disobedient.

A rational conscience allows a child to make appropriate decisions with his peers. At age ten he usually can change rules if all of the children vote for the change. He will abide by the rules, because he feels better this way and is showing consideration for those who play with him.

It is at this point that the Golden Rule begins to be a reality in a child's life. He replaces constraint with co-operation and judges his behavior toward others in the light of their behavior toward him. A ten-year-old demonstrated this when she said, "I *could* take some of my nicer dolls to Penny's house, because she did say that we would play house. But she does not have many dolls and her parents can't buy her any more. So I will just take one old one that I like."

In contrast, people with an authoritarian conscience are insensitive to the needs of others. They are blindly obedient to authority. If they are misled by a warped authority, they may soon be judged as the historian Lecky judged Philip and Isabella: "[They] inflicted more suffering in obedience to their consciences than Nero and Domitian in obedience to their lusts."

When the persistent voice of impatient parents has been

buried in the depths of personality, then a young person is at the mercy of a blind morality. As an adult, he soon comes under the judgment that Jesus made of the Pharisees (cf. Mark 7:9–13). These pious people brought hurt to themselves and others through their prejudice and pride. To them, custom was righteousness.

The Law said that a man must not work on the sabbath, even to heal a man who had a withered hand. A modern Jew knows better than that, for he would tell us that the Law was made to preserve life, not to take it away. But there are many Gentiles today who act like some ancient Pharisees. They wish their customs to be upheld, even though other people are hurt by them. When one of their group is moved by love to violate their code, he may be cast aside. If a Sunday school teacher should begin to teach that "God is no discriminator of persons," so far as Negroes are concerned, some of his old friends may no longer shake his hand.

There are other dangers to those who are victimized by an authoritarian conscience. There is a problem of "scrupulosity." This is the symptomatic behavior of a conscience which insists that obscure actions must be repeated again and again. That which was taught to the person as a rigid rule in childhood has now become a general principle of life: "You must *always* do *everything* right." With no teaching concerning forgiveness and repentence, he is never free from guilt.

During the Middle Ages, such persons would go to their priest again and again to confess petty sins. When assured one week that a few penances would bring relief, the person would return the next week, because he feared that some sin had not been confessed before communion.

The Protestant Reformation reduced the abuse of penance, but people are still troubled by overdeveloped consciences. The joys of the Christian's life are sapped by fears that he may have offended someone by something he did or said. The assurance of faith is denied those who are always anxious, never sure that they have done the right thing.

For momentary relief, a person may wash his hands again and again or check the front door lock three times whenever he leaves the house. But the deeper, unseen conscience, developed out of the abuses of childhood, is not appeased. The child was despised, and now as an adult his inner self responds with hatred of others and contempt of himself. Yet he cannot admit this, for he is blind to his soul's deepest strivings. His anxiety attached itself to some object, such as a casual word, a misplaced coin, an ambiguous look. These insignificant things are used to justify the uneasy conscience that is not seen. When we are in the presence of an individual who continually is afraid that some little word might offend us, we often wonder if this person may be secretly guilty of some thoughts or words against us.

Conscience can be devious and deceptive, but it also can be redeemed. Dependence upon God is the only sure way to make the conscience a part of our moral guidance. The conscience, as the apostle Paul experienced it in the commands of the Law, could bring an uneasy awareness of sin without the righteousness that comes alone from God.

Distortions of conscience are removable after the focus of the self has shifted. So long as the ego of man is in control, moral sight will be blurred. Consider, for example, the frequent problem of an inflated self-image. The person who harbors this illusion can see himself only in the most favorable of terms. He is king and his every want is to be supplied. But unfortunately, his pretentions are not based on realistic achievement and people will not heed his demands.

The resultant frustration is intolerable. The kinglike person not only wants his own desires to be first, but he must have gratification without delay. Even the most reasonable of such delays seems an insult to his "majesty."

It is even more difficult to satisfy such a person because he usually moves at a very fast pace. Quickly he flits from one project to another and asks a second question before the first one can be answered. He sprays anxiety and hostility like a loose garden hose with a full stream of water.

When Harry Tiebout first observed this pattern in alcoholics, he concluded that their only salvation was in a surrender of the infantile self that created this vicious cycle of unrealistic demands and resultant frustrations. Attempts to placate or control the inflated ego were helpless. But when the individual recognized himself as God's creature and turned over his churning willpower to a divine being, then there was a new perspective.

The question of surrender is of primary importance to people who know the real or probable difficulties of their conscience. They doubt their ability to make the wisest decisions and they know from experience that their strength does not always measure up to their ideals. It is for these people that the Great Physician came to earth—to heal the sick, to mend the brokenhearted, to redeem those who, like Paul, are helpless in the grip of pride and custom.

The age of accountability.—When does one put off the old man and put on the new (cf. Col. 3:9–10)? Must one wait until he is in desperate straits before he implores God to turn his being into a new channel?

The development of a Christian conscience *can* begin in childhood, for he learns then that God is love. So when a child meets love through his parents, he is prepared to meet the God of love who is revealed in Jesus Christ. All that we have seen in the development of self-initiative, concern for playmates, and an inner voice of praise and blame help prepare one for a new life.

The identifiable change of heart takes place when a person is old enough to recognize the strivings of his conscience as his own. Theologically this is referred to as "the age of account-ability." Until this time, the individual does not have a self so completely formed that he can be held responsible by church or society for the ultimate consequences of his actions.

By adolescence, the self is usually defined as independent enough for responsible moral and spiritual decisions. Conscience and conversion are key terms at this age, for now a person knows right and wrong for himself and has the ability to do something about it.

There are at least three theological aspects of an experience of salvation.

First, there is the ability to think of God as more than flesh and blood. He is not an overgrown parent. The distinction between an earthly, fleshly parent and the Heavenly Father is crucial in adolescence. This is the time when young people know the humanity of their parents and often rebel against it. Some of them join the church at an early age when it is difficult for them to distinguish between an earthly and heavenly parent. They often develop the "frozen faith." In adolescence they begin to question the presuppositions of their early teaching and decisions. They feel that they must either lose their identity and submit to the church or rebel against it completely. This problem is becoming more acute among Southern Baptists as the age of baptism steadily drops into childhood. Over 50 per cent of baptisms in Southern Baptist churches represent children twelve years of age and under.[1]

The problem is further complicated by the second theological characteristic of conversion, which is the recognition of sin as a state of rebellion against God. Such a condition is difficult for a child to realize, for he thinks of good and evil as a disconnected series of disobedient acts. Yet, people are re-

---

[1] Research Study 32, July 1963, Baptist Sunday School Board, Nashville, Tenn., III, 20.

ceived into the fellowship of a church on the childish assumption that conversion means that they will "do a little better," though there is little hope for a true change of heart. Christian faith is not built on an infantile conscience but upon an adult recognition that the surrender of self must precede the development of true character. An adolescent is old enough to understand Jesus' teaching that condemnation from God does not come because we have transgressed the rules of the elders. Condemnation is upon those who will not surrender their lives to their Creator.

Another theological characteristic of conversion is the ability to take independent action and judgment on behalf of God rather than submitting to the wishes of men. James Daniel has pointed out in his study of the religious concepts of children that Primary and younger Junior children follow parents' suggestions because they are expected to do so; whereas, the older Junior is beginning to learn some kind of control of his actions, based on his own understanding.

The question of independent action is closely related to the place of the church in the world. In Russia and East Germany, where the differences between church and world are distinct, Baptist or Lutheran children usually are not admitted to full church membership until the age of eighteen. The congregation rightly assumes that they must know the full price of open Christian faith before they make a public decision.

In Canada and some northern sections of the United States, Baptists receive into membership only those who are Intermediates or older. A minority religious group, they are aware of some separation between themselves and the society in which they live. But in the South, 10 per cent of new Southern Baptist church members may be six to eight years of age. It would be difficult for many Baptist children, or their parents, to think of ways in which Southern Baptist churches and southern culture are different. As one college student put it:

"Why I thought I was just doing what everybody was supposed to do when I joined the church! We thought a kid was strange if he didn't." Under such favorable circumstances, so far as the world is concerned, there is little need for the church to ask about the capability of a child to take independent action or adult responsibility for his faith. He is doing what other good people do and the community will approve.

Guidance Through the Gospel

Christians are often surprised by the extent to which their religious convictions are colored by the customs and circumstances of their generation. Because we are influenced by our surroundings and tend to set standards by our own point of view, it is necessary for us to have some timeless norm as our guide.

Christians find a foundation beyond their own feelings in the biblical revelation. Here feeling and fact are combined. Our living experience of God's redeeming grace enables us to understand many events [2] recorded in the Bible, and the events and interpretations of the biblical record are a guide and inspiration to our own attitudes and actions.

If Christian character is to be based on the quality of life that Jesus lived with his disciples, then we need reliable evidence of the life of Jesus and his impact on others. This we find in the gospel record. It combines both the historical facts of Christ and his church with the personal inspiration of those who met him.

The biblical record as a guide for conscience is based on two assumptions about God. First is the conviction that God participates in the history of mankind. He has revealed himself

---

[2] Since the historical circumstances, world view, and customs of various biblical writers are not our own, we must study their times to accurately understand the events of which they speak and the inspired interpretations which they present.

in the mighty acts of redemption to Israel and in the life, death, and resurrection of Jesus Christ. The church is a continuing history of his dealings with men.

Such a view raises two questions for the Christian conscience: How did godly men act in days past? and, what is the relevance of God's will for our own time and circumstances?

These questions introduce the second assumption—that God reveals himself personally, through inspired prophets, through his Son Jesus Christ, and through his disciples in every age. The perfect revelation, Jesus, combines saving event and personal sacrifice. Historical faith now becomes personal involvement: "What am *I* to do that I may live as a disciple of Christ?" To fulfil this task, we need the dual emphasis of the New Testament on historical reality and personal commitment.

The first of these emphases is in the Gospels. The disciples believed that as bearers of the good news they were to walk in the "way" that Jesus had demonstrated before them. To know God and his will was to know Christ and his way of life, for his life was an obedient molding of thought and action to the form of his Father's pleasure. As his life was the imitation of God, so the life of a disciple would be an imitation of Christ (cf. John 5:19; 13:20; 14:6). The theme is summarized in 1 John 4:17: "As he is so are we in this world."

The Gospel of Matthew presents in detail the training of the apostles in the way of Christ. Luke presents sections from the life of Jesus which are paralleled by similar attitudes and deeds in the apostolic church, especially those of Stephen, Peter, and Paul in their suffering for the way (cf. Acts 6, 12, 21). Imitation of Jesus means the daily bearing of the cross (cf. Luke 9:23).

To be personally involved in Christian faith, a disciple must know how his Lord was involved in the lives of his disciples, his enemies, the poor, sinners, and sick ones upon earth. So that he may know God through Christ, he must know how

Jesus was related to God. To attain this knowledge, pray for guidance and understanding as you study the Gospels.

The second New Testament emphasis is upon the significance of Christ's death and resurrection for our lives. This is the theme of Paul and is found also in 1 Peter and Hebrews (cf. Phil. 2:5–7; Eph. 4:32 to 5:2; 1 Peter 4:1,13; Heb. 4:15; 5:9). The life of a Christian, in Pauline thought, is to have the gentleness, humility, obedience, and suffering of Christ (cf. 2 Cor. 10:1; Rom. 15:3; Phil. 2:8; 2 Cor. 13:4; 1 Cor. 4:11). To have the "mind of Christ" is to consider how our lives may show these spiritual qualities of our Lord.

The combining of Gospel narrative with Pauline dedication teaches us how Jesus lived and how we may apply, by the Holy Spirit, that same quality of life to our relations with God and man.

One emphasis without the other will defeat full Christian living. Monastics in the Middle Ages were so obsessed with the literal imitation of Jesus' earthly poverty and unmarried state that this became the "religious" way of life. The daily life of a married man was not considered to be on the same spiritual level.

Southern Baptists in the twentieth century have sometimes gone to the other extreme. As Professor William Hull has said, we hear many sermons on the cross and the resurrection, but our people almost never hear the specifics of Jesus' life. We can defend the supreme significance of Jesus' death, yet cannot give any concrete explanation of *why* he died, *what* the issues of his time were, *where* he stood, and *with whom* he clashed. Nor are we taught *how* to translate the answers to these historical questions into questions for our day.

If anyone doubts this generalization—and a thinking reader should ask many questions—then consider the 1963 Study of the Level of Factual Bible Knowledge on the Part of Southern Baptists. More Baptists knew about the Passover than about the definition of a parable as the means by which Jesus taught his disciples; more knew that Joseph was sold into slavery than that Jesus spent his youth in Nazareth. (Contrariwise, more knew that Thomas doubted Jesus than that Saul was the first king of the Hebrew nation.)

Our need is for a careful study of the Gospel details of Jesus' life and thought, combined with a willingness to let his Spirit lead us in similar ways today. This can counteract our besetting tendency to generalize. Most of us have grown up in a southern culture, where the romantic echoes of Confederate cavalry hoofbeats set the tempo of our lives. An exact, controlled study of historical or contemporary problems has not been appealing. When this romanticism is combined with stereotyped religious phrases, the result is self-deception.

For example, several years ago a pastor wrote an article for Southern Baptists in which he said that the disregard of human rights was a problem "in other lands." He saw no problem of human rights or civil liberties in America. Yet a few years later, this pastor was surprised to find that his church was picketed because it would not receive Negro members. He had not seen the relevance of his article on human rights to the membership requirements of his own congregation.

It is at this point that we face our greatest danger in the biblical witness to our conscience. We are so prone to apply the Bible where it is convenient and to smooth over those sections that disturb our set patterns of life. As a result, people see no direct evidence that our study of the life of Christ has really changed our opinions or prejudices. I face this problem continually with theological students. They ask, "How can you ask us to study the events of the life of Jesus when we do not know persons who try to live by his example today?" When I question them further, they say that most of their Christian associates in adulthood are trying to get by as best they can. Any questions about current problems are met with the quick assurance that we must conform to the standards of our region. It is tragic to see older men plead for belief in the Bible, when young people can see their conduct compromising the basic teachings of Christ.

How can a man uphold the Bible as a book when he does not practice the justice and mercy and righteousness that it commands?

An answer to this question depends on a thoughtful and systematic study of the Scriptures. We may not find an immediate application of every verse that we read, but much reading will build up a storehouse of information and inspiration for a crucial event when our conscience needs illumination beyond itself. This is the time when biblical revelation and personal surrender in faith are combined. We admit that a decision is beyond ourselves. We do not trust our own emotions or judgment. It is at such a time that some event or saying of Jesus, some struggle or circumstance of biblical history can become alive for us.

The Community of Faith

Bible reading and personal communion with God are not enough to develop mature Christian character. There must also be the discipline of questions and answers from godly people. Insights of our brothers in Christ may help us clarify our own interpretation of the Bible.

Reliance on a godly fellowship can save us from such lonely struggles as those which John Bunyan experienced in his first days of conversion. Burdened with a sense of personal unworthiness, Bunyan would not reveal to his fellow Christians the struggle of his own soul.[3] He was tormented by compulsive thoughts of an evil nature. He quoted Scripture passages to drive away the power of such sin. For two years this con-

---

[3] However, his biographer, Ola Winslow, emphasizes the influence of other Christians on Bunyan's decision for Christ.

tinued. In the meantime, there were opportunities for Bunyan to give a witness for his faith in the informal meetings conducted by his Baptist brethren.

Bunyan felt that he had nothing to contribute. But gradually the urgings of the church led him to say a few halting words in one house. This was the beginning of his preaching ministry. I wonder if he would have ever opened his heart, as he later did in *The Pilgrim's Progress* and other works, if Christians had not cared for him and shown that he was more worthy in God's sight than he was willing to admit.

Some of the same struggles occurred in the early life of Bishop McKendree of the Methodist church in the South. For years, this frontier preacher struggled out of depression into exaltation and then back into depression. His unpublished diary reveals his deep despair, his joy in Christian service, and his shyness in telling anyone of his inner struggle. Gradually the Bishop became a difficult man to know. He withdrew within himself during his periods of "religious blues." One of his close associates during those days remarked that the Bishop might have been much easier to live with had he had a family and some fellowship of his own. He was by nature a loving and sensitive man, who keenly felt the deprivations of his lonely, withdrawn existence.

Conscience can tear a lonely man to pieces. God has not meant that we should be delivered over to our own judgments. The apostle Paul gave specific commandment to the Christian church at Corinth that they should judge one another. This is to be done in the light of God's judgment upon us and the warning that we may stumble and fall in the same way. But it is to be done, so that a man may be delivered from the snare of punishment.

Some of the people who read this book will be suffering from the overburdened conscience of a lonely existence. You may say that your burdens are to be cast upon the Lord alone, but you have neglected the biblical admonitions to share your burdens and shortcomings with a concerned community (e.g., Heb. 10:25; 1 John 1:9). Are you greater than your Lord? He told his disciples of his temptation in the wilderness. How else would they have known of it? He expressed his appreciation for the continuation of his disciples with him through many trials (cf. Luke 22:28) and took them to Gethsemane that they might watch and pray with him. The command to the early church was to bear one another's burdens in the spirit of Christ (cf. Gal. 6:1–6). They were to be relieved of the burden of guilt through confession to Christian friends (cf. James 5:13–20).

Most basic to Christian conscience is the influence of a godly family. The household often conditions the emotional response of a person to the Bible or to Christian teaching. James Bossard and Eleanor Boll found evidence of this as they studied biographies to answer questions on *Ritual in Family Living*. They found the autobiography of Stannard Baker revealing a delight in religious services that were part of a happy home in which the needs of the children were given consideration. They also found some unhappy examples, such as the autobiography of Augustus Hare. He described Sunday worship and Sunday afternoon devotionals as rituals that were thoroughly satisfying to his mother but sources of continual agony to him as a child. His cold feet in church and his boredom in a straight chair on Sunday afternoon were of no concern to her.

We need more exact studies of the way in which family patterns influence an individual's interpretation and selection of scriptural passages and truths. Negatively, we can find examples of persons who are stunted in their Christian capacities because they were deprived of affection and attention in their own homes. Chaplain George Bennett looked for evidences of love, trust, and concern among some of the most suspicious patients to whom he ministered at Central Hospital,

Anchorage, Kentucky. He found these people so mistreated and deceived since childhood that they could only respond to him through the set patterns of rigid religion. So long as he related to them formally as a pastor who listened or a preacher who taught, they could continue to see him. But any feeling of tenderness, either on his part or theirs, was a source of such discomfort that the patient would refuse to see his chaplain for a period of weeks or months.

On the positive side, Roy W. Fairchild and John C. Wynn report in *Families in the Church: a Protestant Survey* that parents who taught Sunday school were concerned that their children learn the meaning of fellowship and discipline as well as the factual information about the Bible. Parents who did not teach in a Sunday school seemed more desirous that their children receive biblical information.

For some persons the church will be the family in God—the spiritual home, where there is love and understanding, teaching and discipline (cf. Mark 3:31–35, Philemon 1). Ideally, there should be a unity, an interdependence of biblical, personal, and family witness as channels of the Holy Spirit. Home, church, and Christian history can enlarge the horizons and increase the capacities of people to respond to God's will. But the individual must make an inner decision to keep his own self as center or to surrender himself to Jesus Christ, as he has learned of him from parents, church, and Bible study.

3
Stages in Christian Growth

In the previous chapter, we considered the major guidelines for Christian growth: a transformed conscience, the biblical record, a redemptive church and/or family. Now we will direct these to the self-development of a convert and see how a new conscience emerges from a surrendered self, how the church can be the good soil in which a fragile child of God becomes a stalwart man in Christ, and how the record of Jesus' life and the thought of Paul provide example and wisdom for the growth of Christian character.

Each of these tasks may be viewed as stages in Christian development. There is first a preoccupation with self, the turmoil of deciding what one is to think or do as a new man in Christ. In the midst of this uncertainty, a Christian conscience becomes a source of inner stability.

Second, a growing convert moves from his self-preoccupation to a consideration of the fellowship with which he is identified. He recognizes the support of the church and seeks its guidance.

Third, a maturing man in Christ sees that the life of Christ must be his supreme guide. The church is helpful, and his inner conscience is a good warning, but these are human guides and are not infallible. True maturity comes when a man can judge both himself and the society in which he lives by the spirit of Christ.

These stages blend into each other and should never be thought of as independent. For example, we have already seen in the previous chapter that family, society, and church have much to do with the development of conscience. So the first stage of my outline, preoccupation with self, presupposes church and family influences.

Also, any one of these stages may come before another. I am not suggesting an absolute order for Christian growth. There are no studies to justify such a scheme. I am presenting my impressions about growth in grace in a convenient way for teaching. My hope is that at some future date there will be a more reliable and specific study, prompted by my educated guessing.

The Surrendered Self

The initial struggle of the adult convert is to reform himself. Old patterns of life must be abandoned or transformed by the Holy Spirit. There is much instability because the egocentric configurations of a lifetime must be changed. The battle will go on for a long time, as the assumptions of unregenerate living are reoriented. This kind of struggle will be most severe in the adult who has been far from Christian faith and church or who has never concerned himself enough to even attend a church service. The contrast between former and present way of life is obvious. A decision for Christ often brings a clear search for new identity.

A man who joined the "First Church" during a revival service stated that his decision was very difficult, adding: "I was a tough nut to crack, but I have been saved from the time I walked down that aisle and humbled myself and confessed my sins and asked God to forgive me. I don't make a move now without consulting the Master. Even before I bought this house I prayed that God would prevent the deal if it wasn't right. This decision made a new man of me." So great a faith does bring reward.

Salvation has a new quality in life for those who have experienced failure and frustration. For example, Mr. S. said that before his decision he seldom thought of Christianity, but that it had become the most meaningful thing in his life. He had returned from failure in another state and was job hunting in town, but he was unsuccessful. The family lived on borrowed money. The Christmas before the revival was a barren one. Moreover, he and his wife were "always fighting." He stated, "We argued all the time. When I made my decision though things began to change." Mr. S. knew that he wasn't alone any more. Six weeks after his decision he found a job which he still holds. He believes that his family is "closer and happier" and he and his wife have learned to forgive each other.

These are some of the testimonies from converts who were still active in a church one year after their conversion during a revival service. These men and women looked for a reshaping of themselves. As Liston Mills studied their decisions, he concluded that the mature ones were seeking to become "new men" in at least four ways.

First, they were stronger individuals. Instead of "going to pieces" when a crisis arose, they maintained some balance and perspective. They also had some control of their impulsiveness, as when a husband restrained his desire to buy a new car and came home to ask his wife what was really needed most in the household. There was a sense of self-respect in these people because they believed themselves significant in the sight of God and his people.

Second, there was a more secure sense of salvation. One woman reported that she felt "more at ease" and did not fear "backsliding" as much as she had. She felt that this decision was different from former ones in that now she was moving toward God on her own, not because of pressure from other people. Furthermore, she believed that the people in the church were friendly and that they had not been "pushy" in trying to get her to join.

Third, there was a sense of loyalty and durability of commitment. Some of these converts had become responsible leaders in the congregation. Junior and adolescent converts, who had no church offices to hold, were faithful in their attendance at church services. There also seemed to be strength with which they could meet some of the trials and temptations of their daily lives.

Fourth, these people were increasingly sensitive to ethical values and were willing to take responsibility for moral living. One man commented: "I have committed every sin I am big enough to—I am a sinner, but God saved me and he did it all over." Mr. G. continues to be convicted of sin in his life, for he says, "I have been convicted of a lot of things as wrong that I used to think were all right." He has quit using profanity at work and has explained to other men that he has been saved. He has assumed several positions of responsibility in the church.

The integration of self in the image of Christ usually proceeds through several stages. The persons who have just been quoted were in the initial stage of Christian character and were preoccupied with the reformation of their inner attitudes and the ability to stay away from sin. In some respects the adult convert is like the new member of Alcoholics Anonymous. The great preoccupation of the latter is to remain sober. If we were to talk to a member of Alcoholics Anonymous, he would probably describe such a person as "trying most of all to dry out." Much support is given by members of the group as a new man or woman tries to keep away from alcohol for one day at a time.

The Secure Fellowship

A new self is fragile. Like the alcoholic, a convert may be happy with his new sense of peace and still wonder how long it can continue. One man described the ups and downs of a self-change in this way:

I can be more at peace with myself. Before . . . I couldn't sleep some nights, things were unsettled. Now, since the decision, I can relax. When I was fourteen I didn't feel a real forgiveness like I did last year. I have talked to some people I wish would make a decision and I have done some work on the building, but I still lack confidence in myself in church work.

To develop character, the convert needs a school in Christian living. This he may find in a church. His initial surrender is a bid for companionship, as we may see in the following confession: "I feel like it was necessary for me to confess my sins before God and the congregation. I had come to the point I couldn't reach God, but when I got the courage to walk down the aisle I felt it lift. I felt like I was going up and asking God to forgive me my sins."

Man learns what faith is in a faithful community. When people are gracious to him, then he begins to understand what grace can mean in his own life. At this stage in his development, a Christian may become very dependent upon the church organization. He is there "every time the doors are open." For persons who are moving from worldly company into Christian faith, some faithful fellowship is essential. John Wesley saw this when he organized Saturday night class meetings for his converts in England. Conditions were so bad in eighteenth-century England that a convert *had* to go to class meeting on Saturday nights. The only alternatives in a godless society were drinking and debauchery. Family life was chaotic and housing conditions were unspeakable.

Whatever the social conditions, Christian fellowship is a channel for the growth of character. But it cannot be fellowship for the sake of fellowship.

A redemptive church is more than a social club of congenial citizens. The New Testament looks upon the fellowship as a channel of God's grace rather than the very source of satisfaction itself. The source of salvation is Christ revealed in his spirit (cf. Eph. 4:1–16; 2 Cor. 13:4; 1 Cor. 12:13). As we have seen in the previous chapter, our own character and our culture must be conformed to the biblical witness. It is through adherence to Christ's example that we learn the meaning of fellowship between man and man and between man and God (cf. Matt. 18:21–35).

The appeal of God is made through our fellowship (cf. 2 Cor. 5:20 to 6:10). In love for one another we imitate God (cf. Eph. 5:1–2). Our ability to understand and sympathize brings conviction to the hearts of unbelievers (cf. 1 Cor. 14:23–25).

The church that honors Christian citizenship will be a partnership of all who share common devotion to Christ. It will be characterized by the sharing of suffering and the strengthening of those in trouble (cf. 2 Cor. 1:5–7; 1 Cor. 12:26; 1 Peter 5:9–10; James 5:13–18; Rom. 15:1; Gal. 6:1–6). The priesthood of believers is the ministry of Christians to one another. Individual reformation is built on redemptive relationships, divine and human.

Although the church is the agency that is to stimulate spiritual growth, it sometimes erects barriers to the individuality which it should promote.

One of the chief barriers is conformity to social custom and unquestioned acceptance of theological presuppositions. Since the church is part of the larger community, it tends to take on the social coloration of the dominant members. As Will Herberg has pointed out in *Protestant-Catholic-Jew,* indentification with a church is more a sign of "belonging" in society than it is surrender to a set of religious beliefs.

Usually the convert takes a step up the social ladder when he joins a church. For, as Jerome Davis, in 1928, found in his study of the churches of seven denominations,[1] "On the whole the membership of the boards of control is made up over-whelmingly of the favored classes."

Even when a church makes an effort to win members who come from a lower or higher "social level," it is an uncomfort-able relationship. For example, one man who joined First Church had recently moved to the city from a rural area. Neither he nor his family knew how to get along in the new community where he served as custodian of a school. Soon he was in trouble, for in his own words, "I fell in with the wrong crowd when we moved to town."

A friend confirmed this judgment and said that Mr. C. and his family had little culture and were very poor, but they did join the church during a revival and this decision helped to keep Mr. C. away from the wrong company. At the time of the decision he was very happy and "wanted to shake the hand of everybody in the church." But in a short while he began to stay at home on Sunday. When asked about this a year later he said, "They never gave me any part to play. Certain ones up there have too much to say."

Mr. C.'s friend observed, "They never really became close to anybody in the church. Our church isn't the type that would keep on and make you feel welcome." Uncomfortable from the beginning, Mr. C. did not find the continuous, spontaneous, and hearty welcome to which he had been accustomed in his former way of life. He is now an inactive member.

A social class would not be as great a factor in a church if it

---

[1] "The Social Action Pattern of the Protestant Religious Leader," *American Sociological Review*, February, 1936, pp. 105-44.

were not for the blind conformity that goes with it. Instead of
a stimulus to thoughts and questions, conversion has become
for many the sign of unquestioned status. No one probes the
convert about his motivation for becoming a Christian, and
he asks no questions of anyone else in turn. Everything is
settled, or settling.

Under such conditions, people who do have questions are
afraid to voice them, lest they should be rejected or tarnish
their status. But the questions remain. When I assisted a pastor in an inquirer's class for prospective church members, we
found that two-thirds of the people at the first meeting were
already members of the church. Some of them had been members for years and several were Sunday school teachers. These
quickly explained that they wanted to sit in with "the in-
quirers" because they had many questions about the Christian
faith that had never been answered in their years of church
membership. They felt that they would look foolish if they
asked these questions in their regular church organizations.
As one woman said, "We never have a chance to ask questions
anyway." How can a convert develop individuality when he is
held in the dependent attitude that was prevalent in that
congregation?

A second barrier to personal growth is superficial preaching.
The church, where an individual should receive instruction
in the faith, sometimes leaves the convert more frustrated
than filled. If a minister were systematic in his preaching of the
New Testament, he would have as many messages on Christian growth and character as he would have on conversion.
My interviews with thirty-five Protestant pastors in one city
revealed that only two or three of these men took time for a
systematic biblical preparation of their sermons. Most of them
stated that the press of administrative and pastoral duties
prevented their reading and thinking as they wished before
they must preach. As a result, indiscriminate exhortations to

repent have taken the place of biblical instruction on growing in grace. When I asked church members for their reaction to this kind of preaching, they usually shook their heads in resignation and said, "Well, we usually do not get much from the sermon, but our minister is sincere and he is a wonderful Christian man. Besides, we should be here for the sake of our influence."

With so little food for spiritual development, it is no wonder that a Gallup poll of 1964 listed "habit" and "duty" as the first two reasons persons attend worship services with some regularity.

The church can also inhibit individuality by "fixing" a convert at the stage of organizational dependence. It is good for the church to encourage and watch over the attendance of a new member at meetings designed to support and direct his Christian character, but attendance upon organizational meetings should not be the central theme of approval. Activity, no matter how pious it may be, is not to be worshiped for its own sake.

In fact, the vain repetition of church activity may bring little benefit to some beyond those of "duty." For example, to again cite the 1963 study of factual Bible knowledge on the part of Southern Baptists, the scores of some who had attended Sunday school for twenty or thirty years were sometimes lower than those who had attended Sunday school for three to seven years.

The Mature Man of God

In the final analysis, a new sense of identity must be guided by the biblical record of Jesus' way of life. Neither the individual nor the church community is completely reliable. In the Gospels we find the evidence and the inspiration from Jesus' resolution of the conflict between his own identity and the demands of the community.

As Wayne Oates has pointed out in *Christ and Selfhood*, it was necessary for Jesus to establish his identity in relation to his own human family. He was respectful of his parents, but he told them that the Temple was his Father's house (cf. Luke 2:49). At the age of twelve he had already made the distinction between a heavenly and an earthly parent. Later, when his family did not understand his mission and came for him, he replied, "Who are my mother and my brothers? . . . Whoever does the will of God is my brother, and sister, and mother" (Mark 3:33-35).

Jesus taught that those who identified with him might have a similar struggle with their own families (cf. Matt. 10:34-39). He who would be great in the kingdom of God might have to be least in the eyes of his own family.

Yet, this teaching on responsibility of a disciple to the larger family of mankind did not mean that Christians had no further need of family companionship. Jesus often used the model of parent-child relationships to explain the marvel of God's dealings with men. The very plan of redemption of mankind was presented as the story of a wayward son and a patient father (cf. Luke 15:11-32).

A mature Christian is to be a responsible son or daughter, wife or husband. But Jesus taught that such maturity would come only when an individual is willing to give up dependence on his parents in order to identify himself with the Heavenly Father.

The life of Jesus also illuminates the conflict between a new self and the larger community of mankind. Jesus recognized the traditions, customs, and legalisms of his own people. He commented on the interpretations which the "men of this generation" made concerning his behavior and that of John the Baptist. Their customs were different, and the opinion of the people was therefore confused (cf. Luke 7:31-35).

When the practices of his day did not conform to the basic

intent of God, Jesus disregarded them. He was not opposed to the plucking of grain by a hungry disciple on the sabbath, and he defied the Pharisees by healing the hand of a man on that day (cf. Mark 2:23 to 3:6).

Jesus sought to free his disciples from unnecessary dependence on the customs of the day. "If the Son makes you free, you will be free indeed" (John 8:36). In his own town, Nazareth, he preached a sermon on the works of God among those who were not their Jewish ancestors. His neighbors were infuriated and would hear him no more (cf. Luke 4:14–30).

Jesus clashed with his community only when his identity and message must be maintained. On other occasions he co-operated with whatever the custom of his time required. He went to the synagogue, he paid the Temple tax, he attended the great feast, he fulfilled the Law. It is not necessary, therefore, that a man define his character by continual isolation or belligerence.

The community is valuable, and as the apostle Paul has written, we are to live peaceably with all, "so far as it depends upon you." We are indebted to parents for their nurture and admonition and to the church for comfort, instruction, and fellowship. But there may be times when an individual will stand against family or the organized church for the sake of his view of Christ's message.

The apostle Paul strove for this kind of maturity. Especially in the midst of church dissension, he was determined to know nothing except the cross of Jesus Christ. When there was a question between his own views and the views of those in the church, he sought to relate both views to the mind of their Lord. In the process he wrote a paragraph that relates conscience to community (cf. 1 Cor. 4:1–5).

The apostle recognizes that he is judged by the community to which he belongs. But that judgment is nothing compared to the righteous sentence of God himself: "But with me it is a very small thing that I should be judged by you or by any human court" (1 Cor. 4:3).

Both here and on other occasions the letters of Paul demonstrate his independence of society. In the letter to the Romans he argued the superiority of freedom in Christ over his former slavery to the Law. He had been set free from the social customs of his people. In another letter, he asked the Colossian church members why they adopted so many human precepts and doctrines when they had died in Christ to these elemental spirits of this world (cf. Col. 2:20–23).

Paul was also aware that his conscience must struggle with his inner convictions. Therefore, he went on to write, "I do not even judge myself. I am not aware of anything against myself, but I am not thereby acquitted" (1 Cor. 4:3–4). The apostle already knew the dangers of personal impulses that override an individual conscience. In his preface to the Romans he said, "Though they know God's decree that those who do such things deserve to die, they not only do them but approve those who practice them" (Rom. 1:32). He felt that an inner conscience was valuable and that it was a source of condemnation or approval for the self. Gentiles who showed what the law required in their hearts were accused or excused by their conscience (cf. Rom. 2:15).

But personal approval or rebuke was not enough. Paul knew the blind Pharisaism of his former life too well to trust his own conscience. Even with the redemption of Christ, he found himself powerless to do what his own best self required: "For I delight in the law of God, in my inmost self, but I see in my members another law at war with the law of my mind and making me captive" (Rom. 7:22). He could not do right in the strength of his own conscience, even when he approved the action he should take.

Therefore, although he took the inner conscience quite seriously, Paul recognized his limitations and he was no more bound by it than he was by any human court, for he had surrendered his will, the opinions of others, and even the mighty binding power of the Law to a superior rulership of Jesus Christ. It was in the Lord he now rested his case. Not the conscience but God was his guide. This submisssion to the judgment of a just and loving Father brought him freedom from the tyranny of his own judgment and the blind prejudices of his culture. He could stand against the churches, when necessary, for the cause of Christ; and he could live at peace with men, when necessary, for that same cause. Maturity for him was to press on beyond personal ambition or community approval to the upward call of God in Christ Jesus (cf. Phil. 3:12–16).

4
Guilt and Forgiveness

The formation of Christian self-identity is not a placid process. As our personality integrates about Christ, we know more about shame and humiliation. Shame and selfhood are closely related. Personal maturity does not remove all guilt; instead, we learn to feel guilty about deeper things.

Paul urged his readers to move from an immature preoccupation with external customs to a mature concern for loving relationships. This is the true spirit of one in Christ. We stumble and fall as we seek this maturity. Because we are fallible, imperfect, we must not only consider the Christian standards for mature guilt but also the Christian experience of forgiveness. The release from past negligences, through forgiveness, is necessary for us to obtain new life for further spiritual growth.

Learning to Be Ashamed

A redeeming sense of guilt is the storm warning of the soul. Since old patterns of life may obscure or change it, it is necessary to know why we feel guilty and what we should do about it. An appropriate stirring of conscience is a guide to Christian character.

The first teachers of guilt are parents. A mother will praise her child for sharing a toy or rebuke him for biting a playmate. Gradually the child imitates the feelings of his parents. As we have seen in the previous chapter, this is the molding of his conscience. "Mama said" is the ultimate moral command of a five-year-old.

In school a boy learns that his friends have rules which must be followed if the game is to be fun. Just as he is shamed and rejected on occasions at home, he experiences the same with his friends. So they become teachers about guilt.

In late childhood and early adolescence, the individual thinks of shame and guilt in light of his own moral choices. He is not as vulnerable to the rejection of others as he was at an earlier age. Now he is more sensitive to warnings from within.

What does one hear from within? The child with an authoritarian conscience is afraid of breaking a thousand rules. He has been taught to emphasize external conformity to the will of his parents. When he misplaces an object or makes a conspicuous mistake he is distressed. But little has been shown him about the withholding of love and consideration for others. He does not know how to feel guilty for that.

Another child may be encouraged to look for the motives behind actions. He can explain why people do things differently from him, and he knows some independent reasons for his own convictions. He may be mildly troubled if he misplaces a piece of clothing or forgets one daily Bible reading, but his major concern is about jealousy, envy, exclusiveness, or hatred toward people. He knows that a hurt to others is a basic reason for guilt.

Jesus noted the misplacement of guilt when he rebuked the "blind guides" who were very concerned about appearances, but neglected justice, mercy, and faith (cf. Matt. 23). They felt guilty about the wrong issues. In fact, they were so preoccupied with little things that they hardened their hearts against Christ when he healed a crippled man on the sabbath. Jesus looked upon them with anger (cf. Mark 3:1–6).

If we had witnessed this scene between Jesus and the men of his day, we might have asked, "Why do they not feel ashamed of themselves?" Jesus taught that some conspicuous religious leaders of his day had a wrong sense of values. They considered ritual and worldly praise before the alleviation of human suffering (cf. Matt. 12:1–14; 23:1–36). Furthermore, these men knew no shame because they did not know themselves (cf. Matt. 15:14).

A Christian has a new sense of guilt because he has a new purpose in life. The gracious redemption of God has begun the change in his concept of self and others. One convert has given the following testimony:

> I felt empty and mechanical with no future or purpose before the revival. I knew that I couldn't live forever and I wanted something to look forward to. Now, I feel like a human being and not an object running around with no meaning. I am no longer afraid to die. I know that when I have a need, I can call for the pastor or look to the church.

A sense of security with God can give us a steady look at the source of our guilty feelings. To feel the right kind of guilt is to be spiritually alive. It is as much a part of our well-being as sudden pain is a necessity if we are to keep our hands away from a heated electric plate.

Known and Neurotic Guilt

A reliable sense of shame guides the man who knows himself and is at peace with God. In fact, it is his relation to God that may often be the first signal of sin. Inability to pray, lack of joy in religious exercises, a vague spiritual uneasiness may be the storm warning. Disquietude toward God may show that something is wrong in a man's relationship to himself or to other men. The young man in the following interview began to sense just this kind of discomposure on the eve of his wedding day.

YOUNG MAN: I don't know why I have felt so uneasy about talking with you. After all, it's routine for couples in the church to see you before marriage, and that's why I am here. But I have worried for days about this interview. . . . Coming here to the church and being in the minister's study all makes me think more about the seriousness of this thing and the purity of the girl I am going to marry and, well, I do not know if I am worthy of her or not.

PASTOR: Is there any reason why you should not have confidence in yourself—or anything about this that relates to God?

YOUNG MAN: I think I should have talked to somebody five years ago when I got into a little mess with a girl. It didn't seem like so much after a little while and I forgot it. At the time I felt very unworthy and stopped going to church altogether. I guess I have just wandered around with that thought loose in my mind, but—ha, ha—now I am really going to be tied down.

PASTOR: This is what worries you?

YOUNG MAN: Well, I mean I ought to get everything off my chest before I marry a girl like this. And besides, I would like to come back into the church myself, but I guess I just needed to tell somebody about this feeling. I never got any other girl in trouble—except that one time—and I wish that would never have happened. I guess both of us were looking for the same thing, and now I don't see it the same way. I want to be a better man than that.

PASTOR: That's possible if you can be completely unburdened of this rankling secret. It sounds as though there has been some change of heart about the way you used to live.

YOUNG MAN: I tell you, Preacher, I am not very proud of the way I used to act, but I thought I ought to tell somebody—and, well, someone who knows about religion and those things.

PASTOR: You think there has been some change and you need some assurance that God recognizes this?

YOUNG MAN: Well, yeah.

PASTOR: And that you can go into this marriage forgiven for past sins?

YOUNG MAN: That's right. You know I am marrying a fine young girl and I met her family and—well, I guess my confidence was a little shaken in myself. It makes me feel better to know that you take these things seriously and—well, I do want to come to church with a clean conscience.

This man was willing to look squarely at his insecurities and their cause. The contrast between the pure relationship of the present and the sordid relationships of the past made him uncomfortable enough to talk openly with a pastor. As a result, his sense of guilt was lifted and he entered marriage with a godly confidence.

In contrast, another person came to the pastor with a complaint that sounded the same on the surface. She had some vague feelings of unworthiness. But as she continued to talk, it became apparent that almost all of her relationships were unsatisfactory. She spoke of her nervousness around her son: "He is not as perfect as I once thought he was. I have been disappointed in him. I have been disappointed in myself."

PASTOR: Well, perhaps there is something to be said on both sides.

MRS. M.: That sounds like my husband!

PASTOR: Have you talked this over with him?

MRS. M.: No, he wouldn't understand like you do.

Mrs. M. gave detailed descriptions of fights with her husband and with various citizens in the town. Most of them took place through snide remarks at cocktail parties or gossip over the phone. Finally she said: "You see our families fight all the time. I got pregnant before we were married a year. I couldn't stand it. I used to take off for J'town to get away from it. That's when I met Dr. E. No one knows about the affair but my dear husband. He's most understanding, but it is all a front. Well, I am keeping you. I must go."

PASTOR: You seem to have made a confession.

MRS. M.: Oh, I really fell in love with that man. I felt so faint when I saw him on the street the other day that I had—well, I know that my physical pains are all because of this conflict. I was so nervous I couldn't drive the car. It would take me hours to tell about it.

Mrs. M. will need many hours with someone who knows how to unravel the rationalizations of a neurotic person and help her to look squarely at some of the basic deprivations of her life. This will be no easy task, for Mrs. M. has a lifetime of self-deception. Unloved and unwanted since childhood, she has compensated with beauty and brashness. She often feels guilty, but her feelings do not lead to a resolution of her problems. Why? Because she is continually sidetracked by some unconscious method of concealment. She does not know herself as a middle-aged woman with too much make-up and too little sincerity. Instead, she talks of her guilt as though she were a charming young woman engaged in an occasional flirtation.

Mrs. M. demonstrates one popular reaction to guilt—concealment. She resents her son because he is no longer under her domination and she loathes her husband, because he is not the man she expects him to be. But in her eyes these are incidental problems in comparison with her numerous infatuations and her vague physical complaints. As Lewis Sherrill has described this *Guilt and Redemption*, she has thrown responsibility for her actions upon others and has invented reasons to justify the way she feels. Anxiety, anger, and guilt are mixed together.

Concealment of the real cause—hatred of others—cannot smother the guilt. It begins to appear either physically, as a distress that physicians cannot cure, or psychologically, as a projection of complaints upon others.

When such a person is "made to see" his mistakes, there is a furious rejection. Deep inside himself, a voice says, "You are never wrong" or "Admit nothing, for your enemies seek to harm you." These words are so beclouded by excuses that they never become conscious faults. On the surface, the person says to us, "Why, *I* am not guilty. You just do not understand what I am up against."

Some people do not even try to make up excuses. They just drift along with their guilt. This is a second reaction to sin. It is a lack of concern, the sign of an undeveloped conscience. Hobart Mowrer, research psychologist at the University of Illinois, believes that many people are neurotic because they are not sufficiently concerned about the best impulses that move them. Instead of obeying the realistic voice of conscience, these people "sell themselves short." As Reinhold Niebuhr has written in *The Nature and Destiny of Man*, they commit the sin of being less than a self. Such persons are devoted to particular desires that perish in the using. They are satisfied with sensuality as the center of self (cf. Rom. 1). They are "integrated," but the object of their integration, self-satisfaction, makes them sick.

Anton T. Boisen described a third outcropping of guilt in his *Exploration of the Inner World*. This is the reaction of withdrawal from others. Sometimes it is so extreme that a person cuts off all normal relationships and may need psychiatric treatment before he can be restored. Or it may be a transitory fling of depression, because of an overwhelming sense of guilt. When we cannot endure this after a few days, the guilt can be resolved through confession. Then relationships can be restored.

At other times the guilt may lead to a chronic withdrawal from society. For example, a woman was divorced at age twenty-five, did not re-enter a church until she was fifty because she felt that "people would look down" on her. She had been taught that divorce was unpardonable. In her church a person could not teach a Sunday school class or serve on any committee if divorced. This was *the* sin.

Because of what she saw in such attitudes, the woman wanted to hide from anyone who knew of her personal failure in marriage. It was not until her church changed its attitude toward persons who had made such a conspicuous failure that she was persuaded to come out of her home on Sundays. And several years went by before she could again talk comfortably with friends.

The development of Christian character is aided by a more open confrontation of guilt. This fourth reaction is aided by forthright questions, such as, "Is this an honest mistake which has brought grief to someone?" If we find that we have acted within the limits of our knowledge to make the best decision that we could, then we will not be overwhelmed by guilt. We will be sorry for the consequences but will recognize that it is no sin to be human, that is, to be limited in foreknowledge and in judgment.

Sometimes a distraught parent will say, "If only I had *known*," when a child becomes seriously ill after showing some

minor symptoms of discomfort. But the original symptoms may
have been so vague that it would be difficult for anyone to
make a diagnosis. The parent did what he could when he
saw serious signs. If he then took appropriate action, he has
acted within the best capacities of a human being. We are
not God, and we can neither foresee nor prevent some tragedies.

This explanation should be most acceptable to regenerate
persons who have acknowledged the finitude and surrendered themselves to God, the source of all wisdom and power.
Christians sometimes try to express the result of this relationship when they say: "I must accept the will of God." Such
a statement needs investigation. If a person means that he
is limited in strength and understanding, then he can receive
Christian comfort. We cannot fathom the mystery of suffering
and evil, but we do know that our God is with us in our
time of distress. On the other hand, some persons use "God's
will" in a fatalistic sense. They believe that God has decreed
this particular misery to teach them a lesson or to punish
them for sin. Although there are Old Testament passages
that support this view, Jesus taught his disciples that individuals are not singled out by God for specific catastrophes in
this life (cf. John 10; Luke 13:4-5). *All* are sinners and will
likewise perish—except they repent.

Have our thoughts or actions damaged our relationship
to anyone? If so, why? Both of these questions must be asked,
for there are times when Christian principles require us to
stand against friends or neighbors. If a man is angry with us
because we will not accept the highball that he offers, we can
be sorry for him without changing our position. If people
threaten or reject us we still can pray for our enemies. We are
not to violate a principle of Christian conduct just to please
people or make circumstances easy.

This interpretation of conscience is unacceptable to the

followers of "popular" religion. Such a religion has no place
for discomfort. Appeasement is considered to be the best
policy whenever a conflict develops. One pastor made this
position explicit when he said: "We have older people in our
church who would get excited if we disturbed their way of
life. They are not accustomed to racial integration in the
church, so why disturb them?"

Sometimes a "relationship" must be damaged because it
is not of the quality that displays Christ's relationship to his
disciples. For example, the pastor of a church in Kentucky
helped to organize a drive against gambling, even though
prominent members became indignant. "It's part of our customs—and the best people play the horses," they said. Some
members supported the pastor, however. One member observed: "My daughter used to take her religion for granted,
but now she sees that it can cost something." Superficial
relations were worse, but the quality of Christian witness
had become stronger in some lives.

There are other occasions when our thoughts or actions
damage relationships to others for no Christian reason. Then
we are at fault and the guilt is appropriate.

Can a Man Forgive Himself?

When we have injured others for our own sake, rather
than for the sake of Christ, what are we to do? Here we are
faced with a problem beyond ourselves.

Forgiveness begins in God. The major theme of New Testament forgiveness is rooted in justification, the gracious activity
of God who loved us while we were yet sinners (cf. Rom. 5).
Where sin abounds, grace doth much more abound.

When this gracious spirit is appropriated by men, it re-
moves the barriers between man and God and between man
and man (cf. Eph. 2). Human forgiveness begins in God's
forgiveness of our sins. This divine forgiveness creates a gra-

cious spirit within the believer. He who has this generous spirit is now ready to remove the barriers that prevent fellowship with other men.

Jesus was more concerned about the things that stand in the way of fellowship than he was about the rapidity with which we restore good feelings among men. His inaugural message on the mountain was filled with warnings against superficial relationships. We must be cleansed ourselves before we will know how to have pure conversations with our neighbor (cf. Matt. 5:21 to 7:5).

At the same time Jesus connected a pure spirit with right relations. A man who is seeking to find God in the temple should be reconciled to his brother before he brings his gift to the altar (cf. Matt. 5:23–24). The relationship is important, but it must be based upon a forgiving spirit (cf. Luke 17:3–4).

A forgiving spirit is one sign of God's activity in removing our sins. Out of gratitude for our new life, we freely forgive others. Shall we be unmerciful servants, when the Lord has forgiven us so much (cf. Matt. 18:21–35)?

The forgiveness of God is not unconditional. Jesus taught his disciples in the Model Prayer that there is one condition of divine forgiveness, which is our willingness to forgive our fellowmen. It is followed by a severe saying: "For if you forgive men their trespasses, your heavenly Father also will forgive you; but if you do not forgive men their trespasses, neither will your Father forgive your trespasses" (Matt. 6:14–15).

Theologians such as William Temple and Basil Redlich have not thought of God's forgiveness and our forgiveness of others as cause and effect. Rather, they see these as two parts of one spiritual fact. We are extending to others the same graciousness that we have experienced from God.

Such an interpretation means that we pass the same judgment upon our brethern that God has passed on us. We admit that they have hurt us, even as God has shown his grief at our sin toward him. It is at this point that some people draw back. Unconsciously they are so weak that they are afraid to admit that they have been hurt. They act as though they are invulnerable and that it does not matter what a person has done. So long as we pretend to stand aloof, we can neither experience forgiveness ourselves nor forgive others. To admit that we need God is also to admit that we are sensitive persons who are vulnerable to the attitudes and actions of others.

We may admit that we have been hurt, forgive our brother from our heart, and still not be reconciled to him. Perhaps he has wounded us so deeply that our memory is still sensitive. We continue to be somewhat on guard in his presence.

In fact, there may be very good reasons for us to be on guard, for the injuring party may remain as before. When he has been warned several times, he may have to be treated as one who is no longer our brother.

A forgiving spirit does not result in reconciliation unless the offending party is as willing to turn to us as we are to turn to him. The younger brother in Jesus' parable of Luke 15 returned to a father who loved him and freely forgave him. But reconciliation was not accomplished until the son came to himself and returned to his father.

So long as we think that forgiveness depends upon us, we have two strikes against us. The modern emphasis upon "relationships" often leaves us to think this way, and it is in keeping with our own pride. Christian forgiveness requires action by three parties: God, the sinner, and the people who have been wronged. Unless we have experienced the forgiveness of God, we cannot have a true spirit of graciousness that transcends the slights and sarcasms of personal relationships. The removal of inner barriers does not become reconciliation until we let down resentment against another and the person who has wronged us repents of his actions.

Worldly and Godly Sorrow

If we neglect divine forgiveness we may often be self-deceived, despite our remorse over some misdeed. One of our principal snares is the thought that we can earn forgiveness by "doing penance."

John A. Broadus called "repent ye" the worst translation in the New Testament. All the material sacrifices of time and possessions are not equal to a broken spirit before God (cf. Psalm 51:17; Mic. 6:6–8).

Penitent acts are a sign of forgiveness but not a precondition of forgiveness. On the one hand there is a danger of the emphasis upon acts without a spirit of contrition. On the other hand there is danger in great expressions of remorse without any outward signs of an inward change.

The apostle Paul looked for both inner repentance and outward zeal in the Corinthian church members (cf. 2 Cor. 7–8). In chapter 9, he commended them for a change of attitude and for their promise of financial assistance to the poor.

This was "godly grief" on the part of the Corinthian church. It was contrasted with "worldly grief" that produced spiritual death. We may look for several distinctions between these two.

Worldly grief seems to be based upon a view of God as one who counts up our good and bad deeds and punishes us now for our transgressions. "Getting right with God" to some people means little more than the removal of the threat that they will be punished. This is in contrast to "godly grief" in which the principal distress is over the loss of relationships with the Heavenly Father. Our alienation from him, rather than the threat of punishment, is our chief concern.

Worldly grief is more concerned about the renewal of comfortable activities than it is about a change of attitude and actions. "What can I do to get by?" is a typical question. A person is remorseful so long as there is hope that he can get what he wants.

In godly grief, a person does not know if he will be restored to good relationships or not. He casts himself upon the mercy of God and others, wondering how they could forgive him after the way he has acted or thought. If people are slow to restore him, he recognizes that human beings can be hurt and that he must show some changes before they can be secure with him.

Worldly grief has no such patience. Patience and humility would be new requirements for the self. And a change in self-attitude is the third sign of godly grief. The person of Christian character has learned something through the suffering of this experience.

What Can Guilt Teach Us?

Guilt that leads through forgiveness to a redemptive relationship can heighten our sense of personal worth and our sensitivity to the needs of others. This can be illustrated in our view of temptation.

The "babe in Christ" thinks of temptation in terms of something that others force upon him. He may, like Adam, blame sin upon women, or, like Esau, blame it on his brother. In either case there is no recognition of personal responsibility.

There are, of course, times when pressure of others contributes to our own personal downfall. An antidote of this is told about Harold Ickes. On one occasion he was belabored by businessmen who said that his Department of the Interior had a reputation in the past for taking bribes. Mr. Ickes is reported to have replied: "To my knowledge, no public servant has ever bribed *himself*."

On a more mature level people recognize that they are responsible as adults for yielding to their own impulses. As the Epistle of James says: "Each person is tempted when he is lured and enticed by his own desire" (1:14). This level of temptation is the one most often presented by Christians who are satisfied with things as they are. They say, "Let a man's heart be right with God, and everything else will take care of itself." This is an oversimplification of the pressures of society upon individuals and is usually believed by middle-class white Protestants who like the society in which they live. But it does demonstrate one stage in the development of Christian character, when we admit personal responsibility for temptation.

Mature Christian growth leads to a third level of temptation in which we acknowledge our ability to tempt others. This requires an adult view of the self in which we know we have some impact on the world about us. It is a move from self-preoccupation, "staying away from sin," toward the acceptance of social responsibilities and the creation of conditions under which people have the most favorable opportunity to obey God's will. It is a regenerate man seeking a redeemed society.

The most severe condemnation from Jesus was not against those who fell into depravity themselves, but those who led "little ones" to perish (cf. Matt. 18:6–14; 23:13–15).

Peace with God does not leave us at ease among men. Salvation makes us more sensitive to the needs of others. Instead of self-congratulation concerning our own purity, we recognize that wherever there is sin in this world, we are a part of it. William Temple wrote: "Let him remember that these horrible things are there, not because some men are outrageously wicked, but because millions of men are as good as we are and no better." [1]

---

[1] *Personal Religion and the Life of Fellowship* (New York: Longmans, Green & Co., 1926), p. 44.

5

Worship and Prayer

Confession and forgiveness are necessary parts of the Christian life, but only parts. Jesus came not only to call for repentance (cf. Luke 5:32) but also to tell men that they might have life and have it more abundantly (cf. John 10:10). The center of this cleansed and abundant life is the worship of God. This is the privilege of a converted man who has responded to the redeeming act of God in Christ. As a new being in Christ, he may now approach the Heavenly Father.

Jesus taught that a model prayer would begin with the praise of God and the submission of self. One purpose of worship is the praise of God for his mighty acts in history and the personal revelation of himself through his Son. It is an expression of our love for the Creator and Saviour.

Worship leads from the praise of God to the duty of man. The Christian presents his body "a living sacrifice, holy and acceptable to God, which is [his] spiritual service" (Rom. 12:1). Strength for service comes not only from solitary communion but also through the "household of God," to which the Christian is joined (cf. Eph. 2). Worship is intended to build up the body of Christ and to continue the fellowship created by the risen Lord (cf. 1 Cor. 11–14).

Fidelity to Christ is a characteristic of Christian worship.

The experience of dependence in worship must be controlled
by the historical revelation of God through his Son. For it is
only in the spirit of Christ that our prayers are acceptable.

Devotion to God raises the moral life of the believer and
extends his concept of God's love among men (cf. 1 Cor.
14:3, 26–33; James 2:1–17; 1 John 4:7–12). God is to be
worshiped for his own sake, but the experience of his presence
elevates the believer and leads the submissive will into sacri-
ficial service.

Communion with God

A person's attitude in prayer tells what he thinks of God
and himself. In a Christian experience, God reveals himself
as personal and ethical. It is the very quality of God's redemptive nature that is transmitted into the loving actions of his
followers who worship him. Those who stand before him
feel that they have been personally gripped by some great
religious truth. That which they have learned is basically the
same as that which was revealed to the prophets of old and
through Jesus Christ. The worshiper has become a new
knower of old things. It is his new "sense" of religion, applied
to the knowledge of himself, others, or God.

Personal confession is often the first impulse of such knowledge, for the individual sees clearly the holiness of God
and the uncleanness of man (cf. Isa. 6:1–5).

The separation between God and his creation is a characteristic of Christian worship. But it is combined with bold-
ness in calling upon God through Jesus Christ. God shares in
the thoughts and sufferings of men, but it is on the basis of
his holy and righteous love. Men make their wishes known to
God but submit themselves to his will.

This type of communion is in marked contrast to the
"popular religion" of our day. Popular religion assumes that
the purposes of God are those that will make men successful

in their worldly desires. When Professors Louis Schneider and
S. M. Dornbusch studied forty-six best sellers in the field of
religion from 1875 to 1955, they found that E. Stanley Jones
was the only Protestant writer who mentioned sacrifice or
purposes of God that might be contrary to the convenience
of men.

In a survey of Southern Baptist literature from September, 1962, to January, 1963, I found the same emphasis on
secular success. Budgets, buildings, and bulging membership
rolls were written down as signs of godly service. Although
there were occasional articles which warned against this
mood, there were no specific signs of confession or repentance.

Although racial unrest has led to the burning of churches,
the bombing of Sunday school children, and the shooting of
civil rights workers, there have been few statements of repentance by the dominant religious groups in the South.
Instead, it is often assumed that God's purposes are our
purposes. Even though some ministers called for repentance
after the assassination of President Kennedy, others were
calling within a month for "a return to normalcy." One Texas
writer stated that his people were evangelical Christians and
could not be blamed. "They give of themselves and their
possessions to bless their fellowman."

How can people think of the gulf between God and
man when their religious organizations are enjoying the prosperity of this world? After surveying his state, one writer
observed: "It has been our best year so far." Membership and
giving were at an all-time high. He noted that there were a
few obstacles, but he was sure that his denomination could
sweep them away.

The formula of popular religion is: Right belief equals
unlimited credit with God. It is modern magic in which the
worshiper assumes that his call upon the name of God will

get him whatever he wants. The purpose of communion with God is to extract whatever favors are desired by the one who has verbally said, "Lord, I believe." Separation between man and God is assumed to be one of quantity; God has more of what we want. Separation on the basis of quality, that is holiness and righteousness, is rejected. Who can think about confession of sin when he is trying instead to discover some easy plan to gain control of God's will for his own benefits?

A discussion of confession and surrender in worship does not mean that all prayers are to be tearful and remorseful. I have made the emphasis on dependence and repentance because it is seldom a living reality in a "successful" denomination, whether it be Southern Baptists of recent years, the Methodists of the early 1900s, or the Presbyterians and Congregationalists of the eighteenth century.

Worship is a part of an abundant life, in joy or in sorrow. There is pleasure in communing with God for his own sake. It is not necessary to think of God only when we need a gift or relief from sin. Such thoughts are more characteristic of the "magical" religion of our day.

Christian communion with God involves a great deal more than this. The prayers of the early church include petition, intercession, healing, and ordination (cf. Acts 1:24–25; 4:24–30; 6:6; 8:15; 9:10–16, 40; 10:9; 11:5; 12:12; 13:3; 14:23; 16:25; 20:36; 21:5; 22:17; 28:8).

These were public prayers, for the New Testament presents communion with God in terms of fellowship. Although there are some instances of private devotion in the tradition of Jewish worship (Acts 10), the early Christian practice was upon the "daily" breaking of the bread and prayers (cf. Acts 2:46). This was a meal that included a prayer of blessing to God in thanks for the bread and wine. Guests contributed their food to the meal (cf. 1 Cor. 11:21). Throughout the New Testament, communion with God was thought of as a part of fellowship (cf. 1 Cor. 1:9; Phil. 1:5; 2 Cor. 8:4; Philemon 6). The Johannine writings stress fellowship with the Father, the Son, and one another (cf. 1 John 1:3,7). To be in Christ is to be a part of his fellowship, which is sustained by the creative activity of his spirit (cf. 2 Cor. 13:14; Acts 10:44; Titus 3:4–7; Rom. 5:5). The Model Prayer begins, "*Our* Father." A Christian cannot pray as an only child.

This kind of worship as participation is difficult for isolated persons. Such persons can think only of solitary prayer. They take Jesus' warning against superficial piety as an excuse for shutting the door of their lives against anyone (cf. Matt. 6:1–6). They do not read further to see that Jesus followed his command about secret prayer with an open prayer before his disciples. Following that prayer was the condition for its acceptance—that we have the forgiving spirit toward others that God has toward us (cf. vv. 14–15).

But when a person has a secret to hide, he can only think of "secret" prayer. Such prayer is usually self-defeating, unless it leads to an open heart before God and opens channels for fellowship.

For example, a woman came to her pastor several Sundays to ask for prayer. She would not say what the prayer was for, and stated that she could only stay a minute, lest someone see that she was talking to the minister about a problem. The minister guessed that she had some difficulty with her husband, since she was never seen with him at church, although both attended faithfully. She would sit with a younger woman. Frequently they held hands and whispered during the service.

A year later, the woman returned to the pastor's study. This time she came during the week and sat down to talk. She had decided to leave her husband. "I've prayed about this for fifteen years," she said, "and can't stand it any longer." In all that time, she had never told anyone what was bothering her. She thought it was a secret. But her conduct and attitudes showed any observant person that her marriage was empty. Self-deceiving prayer did not bring relief.

Hope began to flicker when an older, motherly woman took a room in her house. One day the "mother" had said: "You must talk to some godly person about these constant quarrels with your husband." She then brought the troubled wife to the church, and waited while the wife told her story to the pastor.

Confession is the bridge between repentance and restoration of fellowship for some. Persons who are overburdened by their sins and isolated in their prayers need the encouragement of friends who confess their own weaknesses.

Sharing must be controlled. The object of common devotion is participation in Christ's spirit. We are not gathered together to see who can brag about the biggest sin or show the greatest hostility against his brother. Such "communion" would be irresponsible.

I sometimes face this problem when students in my pastoral care class evaluate the interviews which others in the class share. One student, Mr. A. was very critical of Mr. C. because Mr. C. did not immediately condemn the conduct of one of his members. Mr. C. told the class he was tired of hearing about condemnation; this was all he had ever heard in the church and at college.

Mr. A. said that something was wrong with a man who thought like that. When I asked him *what* was wrong, he wasn't sure. Then, with some prompting, he told of the way in which his godly father and mother had taught him to reject sin. "But," I said, "Mr. C. was six years old when his father died. You assume that he had the loving family that you had—but I don't believe that he has." Mr. C. nodded assent.

Through responsible confession, these men can learn much

from each other. Mr. A. needs to feel what it is like to be brought up by older brothers, uncles, or friends who barely have time for their own children. Out of this understanding he may be able to enter with love into the lives of deprived people. As it is now, he knows no deprivation and assumes that others have had his advantages. Mr. C. needs to feel some lasting concern from others, so that right and wrong will not be loveless restraints but signs of respect and conviction, born of love.

Personal Commitment

In his letters to the Corinthian church, the apostle Paul faced the conflict between responsible and irresponsible fellowship. To him, the highest work of the Holy Spirit was not a garbled language that arose from personal impulse but the facility of prophecy, whereby the believer might live righteously and thoughtfully in the church and before the world (cf. 1 Cor. 12–14). Those who spoke in tongues edified themselves, but those who prophesied spoke clearly and edified the church.

It requires a good deal of personal commitment to hear someone speak "the truth in love" (Eph. 4:15). But this is the way in which we become mature in the body of Christ. Even as Paul spoke plainly to the Corinthians, so we must speak openly on occasions to each other for exhortation, rebuke, or comfort.

Such conversation is possible when two or more are gathered together in the spirit of Christ. It is through our conversion experience, now continued in the fellowship of the saints, that we receive faith, righteousness, justification, joy, love, peace, and security (cf. Gal. 3:26; 2 Cor. 5:21; Gal. 2:27; Phil. 3:1; Rom. 8:39; Phil. 4:7; Eph. 1:13).

The distinction between a committed and an uncommitted response to the Holy Spirit was seen by Colonial and frontier churches as "orderly" or "disorderly" members. The dividing point in church discipline was the "orderliness" with which a brother worshiped, that is, his willingness to live in Christian commitment to the church and its commands.

When a person lives in "orderly" fellowship, his prayers are social as well as personal. He prays for others as well as for himself. The apostle Paul demonstrated this in his prayers as a part of his letters. He asked for an increase of brotherly love (cf. 1 Thess. 3:12–13), for the maturing of the saints (cf. 2 Cor. 13:7–9), and for knowledge and obedience on the part of believers (cf. Col. 1:9–18). He also let people know what he was up against, as he prayed for personal maturity and for the removal of his individual affliction (cf. 2 Cor. 12: 8–9).

Such devotion is only possible when an individual has surrendered himself to the power of Christ. Then he is willing for the will of God to increase in his own life and for his life to be shared with those for whom Christ has died.

Group Worship

In what ways do these concepts of worship correspond to the thinking of modern churchgoers?

Praise and thanks to God are the most frequently acknowledged purposes of worship among Protestants, according to Philip Hammond's research for his dissertation at Columbia University. The seeking of God's will, becoming a better person, and fellowship with others were also mentioned frequently.

"Participation in Christ" seems to be found more through organized church services than it is through personal devotions. In a study of over eight hundred Presbyterian families, Roy Fairchild and John Wynn concluded "that today's Protestant families do only a minimum of worship as family groups; refer all too seldom to literature prepared especially for family worship; and tend to a vagueness in theological understanding that pervades their household conversation and common life." [1] Seven out of ten families represented in the survey said grace regularly at family meals. Less than one family in twenty read the Bible daily. Two thirds attend church at least three Sundays out of every month. As the authors say, "The common worship of the church, together with its face-to-face relationships there, counts for more in the life of today's families." [2]

A fellowship is often mentioned as a purpose of corporate worship, but people often do not meet their closest friends in church activities.[3] Modern worship does not have quite the intimate nature of the worship in a home, which was the common setting for the New Testament church.

Although personal commitment is a characteristic of the biblical theme of worship, modern preaching services seldom engage the conscious participation of worshipers. Instead, the audience is almost completely passive.[4] One reason for this may be the inability of the worship leader to see the world through the eyes of those who hear him. I find that ministers commonly refer to commitment in terms of church activity, reading the Bible, or praying. Specific examples of commitment in work or other aspects of daily life are lacking. In their evaluation of a minister as preacher, people most often tell me: "Well, he is a good man and very sincere, and sometimes I get a blessing from his preaching."

People in some churches are literally starved for an opportunity to participate in worship as a sharing of experiences and feelings. For example, the men who conducted the research for *Families in the Church: A Protestant Survey* met

---

[1] *Op. cit.*, p. 184.
[2] *Ibid*, p. 186.
[3] Victor Obenhaus, *The Church and Faith in Mid-America* (Philadelphia: The Westminster Press, 1963), p. 65.
[4] *Ibid*, p. 159.

with small groups of parents in many Presbyterian churches and asked for their opinions about the relation of the church to their family. Many times the group met far beyond the two hours allotted for the discussion, for as they said: "This is the first time that the church has ever asked us how we felt about anything." Again and again these parents complained that the church made organizational demands upon them that broke up their family life rather than solidifying it.

When Bible study and prayer groups have been organized on a shared basis, as they have been in some American Baptist churches, congregations have been literally revived.

The ritual of daily worship can clarify goals and convict an individual of their necessity. James Bossard and Eleanor Boll found that rituals put into objective action or words those goals that a family held dear. Many rituals emerged in a trial and error way among preschool children with their parents. They soon became satisfying means of expressing family values and often remained fixed until adolescence. Then the family concentrated on the preparation of the children for the adult world and some childhood rituals were dropped.

Such religious devotions as daily Bible reading and prayer could have similar values if they were geared to the growth of the individual. The reasons for such devotions will vary from age to age and must be clearly discussed and presented if they are to be continued after a person "gives up childish ways." Children may read the Bible primarily out of a sense of duty or fascination with graphic character stories. In adolescence, insistence on the duty of devotion is self-defeating, for the young person is not interested in performing these tasks just because his parents or others require it.

To "give up childish ways," a fifteen-year-old may stop all pretense of devotional times, including church services. How can he be challenged to a higher level of spiritual development? Begin by helping him to face up to the question: "What did Jesus do, and how may I pattern my life after his?" This is a shift from an earlier identity with parents to an identity with one who is greater than parents—the Heavenly Father.

This kind of commitment in worship is built on intimacy with adults who share themselves with adolescents and on opportunities for responsible action. The first is seen in leaders who look at life *with* their pupils rather than standing on a balcony and telling young persons *about* life. The second is found in supervised programs of Christian service, such as teaching Sunday school classes in a depressed inner-city neighborhood.

Unfortunately, adults are anxious about this kind of service when it involves any social disapproval or personal discomfort. Adults want teen-agers to "have fun." But the adolescent Christian wants the challenge of serious activity. How will he know what to pray for, or how to understand the biblical message, apart from some risk and some knowledge of the lure of greed and the apathy of poverty?

An alert adult has seen this and needs both guidance and strength to maintain Christian character. When he is challenged to read and pray with real problems in mind, then he can grasp the relevance of Paul's epistles or look forward to sharing in worship.

But this approach has institutional risks. If adults turn from simplified devotional study to a historical analysis of the biblical message and its relevance for today, there may be a great "falling away." In England this latter emphasis coincided with a lessening of popular attention to the Bible. Many other factors were at work in the secularization of English society, and they are active in our society today.

What are we to do? So long as private devotion and public worship support social conformity, our religion seems to be approved and prosperous. If we apply the devotional life to our current attitudes and circumstances, will many, like some of the first disciples, draw away from Jesus (cf. John 6:60–65)?

This is the problem of combining worship and mysticism with action and the prophetic spirit, a challenge of Christian maturity that we will now examine.

6
The Mystical and
the Prophetic Spirit

Two elements of worship, solitude and service, have been described as characteristics of the mystical and of the prophetic spirit. Mystical contemplation is usually related to solitude, while a prophetic spirit is centered upon service and the world to be redeemed. The ideal of mysticism is "the vision of God." The motivation for the prophet is "the hearing of the Word." The former is typically Anglican or Catholic, whereas the latter is an emphasis of the Reformation tradition.

Although there may be some separation of mysticism and prophecy for purposes of emphasis, they are interrelated aspects of Christian experience. The purpose of this chapter is to show how both contribute to one's growth toward Christian maturity.

William E. Hocking in *The Meaning of God in Human Experience* stated that the mystic is an original knower of all truth—one who has been seized by a power beyond himself. The source of his self-consciousness is the development of a new self in the light of God's love.

Willingness to reflect on the meaning of God in one's own experience is the heart of mysticism. In this sense, reflection is the agent by which the worship of God spreads throughout one's total being. Mysticism as inner illumination is an essential ingredient in Christian growth. Without the inward appropriation of the Word of God, the seed of truth might lie barren upon rocky soil.

How would one characterize mysticism in daily life? Christian mysticism has at least three elements—dependence on God for illumination; a sense of personal involvement or commitment to a new insight; and a sense of discovery or feeling that a general truth has now found specific application.

Occasions for Spiritual Insight

The diary of a pioneer Methodist bishop, William McKendree, illustrates some of the ways in which men are illuminated and inspired by God.

Meditation.—On May 24, 1790, Mr. McKendree recorded his thoughts about the way in which steady men are carried to and fro by different spirits acting upon them. He spent several days trying to work out this particular thought. It began on the morning after he had spent a restful evening in Christian conversation with several friends at his father's plantation. There was no great feeling connected with his thoughts. It was an exercise in the growth of the soul, as Mr. McKendree sought to relate Christian teaching to observable experience. It would be a part of the "comprehensiveness" of a growing faith, which was described in chapter 1.

Scripture reading.—On June 26, McKendree awoke with his spirit "disordered." To gain relief, he began to read the Scriptures and soon "felt heaven all around him." Here was a sense of participation in great truths of religion and the feeling that one is caught up in a spirit of that which has been recorded for our inspiration, guidance, and comfort.

Upsurge of affection.—The third day of June was a "precious sweet morning" for McKendree. After several hours of meditation he wrote, "I cannot tell what I felt. O, what a view I had of the union between Christ and the faithful soul." As he started out for his next preaching appointment, it began to rain. He rode for twelve miles, comforted by the thought of "the union between Christ and the faithful soul." Here was a definite exaltation and sense of union with Christ that is often marked as the sign of a mystical experience. It occurred in an active, socially minded individual who would not fit the characterization of mysticism as a withdrawn and "other worldly" state of being. Mysticism has sometimes been criticized for this latter characteristic. Although *some* mystics may be solitary selves, there can also be a sense of union with God among outgoing people.

Social concern.—After reading the Scriptures on the morning of June 26, McKendree walked from the home where he was staying down to the beach of the Atlantic Ocean. There he watched ships going out to sea. They reminded him of the slave cargoes that were often the merchandise in their holds. A great sense of mourning came over his soul as he thought of the farewells of Africans, torn from their home and family. The abominable cruelty and irrationality of slavery was like a gloomy shade upon his soul. He returned to the house where he was to have breakfast. He sat down with a few brethren and in a short time their conversation helped him to feel that Jesus had come down in their midst.

This experience carried a distinct social conviction. It was not the "religious blues" or psychological depression which overcame Mr. McKendree at times. Instead, it was a specific concern for the cruelty of men to men. Mr. McKendree felt in himself all the impact of distress that was the lot of a Negro slave.

The unexpected vision.—While meditating on the afternoon of June 7, Mr. McKendree began to visualize a delicate human form. The form asked, "Do you know me? You have seen me many times, although not in this way." The words struck the minister with such astonishment that cold chills ran all over him. (He had broken out in a sweat the evening before while preaching.) He desired to hear all that he could from this "sweet vision." A voice spoke in one ear and then in the other, reproving him for his backwardness and filling him with a sense of power. Mr. McKendree wrote: "I blushed and sank as into nothing. The voice ceased and the appearance vanished, but my spirit fluttered, my heart beat, all my powers was [sic] awake and celestial fire ran through every power of my body. True I felt little and mean, but at the same time so strong that if

> Trouble should assail and dangers affright
> Friends should all fail and foes all unite
> I will fear no evil, no danger will I fear
> Nor start from the trial while Jesus is near."

There is no further mention of this vision in the diary. The vision is one of encouragement and personal commitment for an impressionable and dedicated minister. There is no disorganization of personality nor great change of purpose because of what has come.

In this way the experience would be similar to that of J. M. Frost, Southern Baptist pastor and denominational executive. While resting at French Lick Springs on the afternoon of July 17, 1916, Dr. Frost had the distinct and powerful sense of the presence of Christ. He also had a sense of parents and theological teachers in the room with him, though all of them had been dead for years. He did not wish to mention the experience to anyone, but he felt so strengthened by the "real, though invisible," visitation that he did share it with some ministers at a later time.[1]

---

[1] J. M. Frost, "A Visit from the Master—an Experience," *Whom the Preacher Preaches* (Nashville: Sunday School Board, Southern Baptist Convention, 1917).

The Control of Self-Deception

Personal illumination is a source of Christian power and guidance, but only when it is controlled by a realistic knowledge of this world, personal humility, and a community concern.

These three characteristics may be found in the book of Revelation, as well as in Old Testament passages in Isaiah, Jeremiah, and Ezekiel. These criteria helped me as a mental hospital chaplain to differentiate between the biblical sense of revelation and the confused visions of persons psychologically ill.

First, there is the distinction between a realistic and a distorted view of the world. In the book of Revelation, the first three chapters describe the state of churches in the province of Asia Minor. As nearly as we can reconstruct the circumstances of that day, the descriptions are authentic. John, the seer, made a penetrating analysis of the inner life of the churches and the culture that threatened them. This realistic scene precedes the visions and revelations of chapters 4 and following. The message is to a suffering church, and the first three chapters describe who the churches are and how they suffer.

In contrast, a pathological vision has no framework of realism. Actually, the illusion may be an unconscious effort to hide and mitigate a painful reality. For example, one man spoke of the time when Christ supposedly appeared out of a cloud and said, "I call no woman to preach." The man assumed that Christ was now calling him to preach. At first he could see no connection between the command of the voice and his personal circumstances, but after fifteen interviews he said, "That vision came on the afternoon that I found another man at home with my wife. I did not know what to do. All my life I would see and not see, hear and not hear. It's not like me to take action or to say something.

. . . But when the Lord spoke to me out of that cloud, then I had comfort." It was the only consolation for a man so passive and indecisive that he could not rebuke adultery in his own home.

A second sign of a godly vision is personal humility. Although John, the seer, recorded what he had seen, he was not the central actor in the drama that unfolded before him. Instead, he knew his own uncleanliness and powerlessness, and was only persuaded to participate in great things when invited to do so (cf. Rev. 4:1; 22:8-9).

Pathological visions are distorted by self-glory. They are a pitiful attempt to cloak a shattered self with fantastic esteem. Such was the case of a girl in her twenties who believed that she was the reincarnation of the virgin Mary. The thought was so all-consuming that she consulted an obstetrician, who sent her to a psychiatrist. Several weeks later, one of the Southern Baptist Seminary students who worked as a psychiatric aide, said, "I believe I know why she had a vision of being the virgin Mary. She has been abused by others since childhood and has done her share of using others for her own purposes. She is sick and tired of the distrust and insecurity of her family, and now she sees it becoming a part of herself. I guess she longs for purity so much that she finally thought she would be like the purest woman of whom she had ever heard."

A third characteristic of godly revelation is social concern. Again and again, the seer is commanded to write down his visions for the good of the churches. Their anguish and suffering is ever before him and it is a comfort to the churches that God, in the midst of worshiping elders and throngs of angelic beings, hears the voice of suffering saints: "Oh Sovereign Lord, holy and true, how long before thou wilt judge and avenge our blood on those who dwell upon the earth?" (Rev. 6:10).

Anton Boisen found that the moral quality of honest confession and the social sensitivity to the sufferings of others were the inner curative powers of mentally ill people. Mystics like George Fox might see visions and do strange things, but it was all for the love of his saints. In *The Exploration of the Inner World*, Chaplain Boisen contrasted this social consciousness with the self-deception and personal absorption of other patients. Those who sought to conceal their faults from themselves and others destroyed every opportunity that others created to help them. Their visions were motivated by their own sufferings, and some included the destruction of those who had tormented them in the past.

The Mistake of Two Extremes

In the early 1800s, mystical states were commonly connected with the call to preach or, sometimes, to conversion itself. Frontier Baptist congregations often looked for a dream or a vision to signify God's call to service. If it were the initial call of conversion, an individual's testimony was expected to include some cataclysmic experience. On some occasions a person might be rejected if his sense of God's salvation were more serene.

A man was expected to "labor under a call to preach." That is, the call was a direct violation of a man's purpose in life. It was thought that God would use sickness, misfortune, and any mishap to punish one who would not turn about and begin to preach. For example, one man cut his foot with an ax and immediately thought, "This is the judgment upon me for not preaching the gospel." [2]

In reaction against this, early Church of Christ or Disciples evangelists depreciated all religious feeling. The Baptist

---

[2] David Lipscomb, *Life and Sermons of Jesse L. Sewell* (Nashville, McQuiddy Printing Co., n.d.), pp. 25–26.

statesman Andrew Broaddus wondered whether Alexander Campbell had any place for the Holy Spirit in his teaching about conversion. Campbell laid complete stress upon a rational acceptance of New Testament passages on salvation. He rejected sudden and vivid emotional experiences as the vehicle of the Holy Spirit, it seemed.

The tension was heightened between Baptists and the Campbell group by the latter's insistence that motivation for evangelism should come from the influence and teaching of the Scriptures rather than from a direct and personal call from God. David Lipscomb, the founder of a principal Church of Christ college, believed in the obligation to preach, if a man made up his mind to accept it. But there was no irresistible call and no extravagant form in which it was to come.

Perhaps both the Baptists and the Disciples would have been stronger had there been less debate and more listening. Baptists had elevated the emotional element in revelation without consideration for the safeguards mentioned in a previous section of this chapter. Disciples reacted against this by exalting the rational understanding of Scripture passages, without due concern for the emotional impact of the message.

The Mystic in Action: The Prophet

The community aspects of Christian mysticism soon led to prophetic action. Prophecy has the corporate flavor of biblical mysticism.

The prophet thinks in terms of his own generation. He is concerned for the relevance of God's Word to his own people. At the same time, the prophet speaks with a sense of individuality. His revelation is a work of a personal experience with God.

God does not give a revelation without the aid of the world to which he gives it. In creating it, he swathes it in particular historic fact and context. As the Gospel of John expresses the most complete revelation of God, the Word became flesh. In the prophetic tradition, God speaks through the men whom he has created and inspired.

The task of the prophet is to present his personal experience with God to the world. His insight carries the impact and identity of his own personality. This is the limiting and circumscribing quality of a historical revelation. But it is intended that the revelation should be historical; the prophet is seeking in daily living to make a reality of God's judgment upon world events.

The Price of Prophecy

In the creative act of revelation, God moves an inspired man to a historic deed. William E. Hocking calls this the supreme moral achievement. Certainly it demands Christian maturity, for wisdom, humility, and patience under suffering may be the lot of a prophet.

Hardship attends the Christian who is impelled to apply God's love to entrenched injustices. In Kentucky, the North District Baptist Association charged Elder David Barrow in 1802 with "meddling with emancipation" and thereby disturbing the peace of the church. Elder Barrow apologized for disturbing the Association and charges were dropped. But at the next yearly meeting, ministers reported that the Elder was still preaching gradual emancipation of slaves. The Association expelled him and sent a committee to his church at Mount Sterling to prosecute him. The church stood by their pastor and refused to send messengers to the next meeting of the Association. After fighting Elder Barrow, the churches of the Association began to fight each other and soon declined. Elder Barrow spent most of his life thereafter in an unsuccessful attempt to influence Christians in his state to emancipate their slaves, but his "brethren" were not with him.

Forty years later, John Fee became pastor of a church in

Louisville which had only one slaveholder. She was the widow of a former pastor. The church was pleased with his preaching but requested that he sever connection with his parent presbytery in Cincinnati because it was tainted with abolitionism. He refused and was denied the pulpit. Then moving to Lewis County, Mr. Fee organized a church and preached a sermon on slavery as contrary to the Word of God. A wealthy slaveholder denied his pledge of twenty-five dollars toward the church after hearing this sermon. Fee continued to preach as best he could to the eight or twelve persons who would hear him. In 1845, his synod in Paris, Kentucky, told him that he was violating the "peace of Zion."

Mr. Fee observed that the majority of ministers acknowledged the wrong of slavery but said it was to be worn out by much preaching. They were negative in their attitude and conservative in their approach to social problems. On the other hand, the slave power was positive, aggressive, and able to override the conservative ministers and their churches. Mr. Fee, therefore, decided that nothing short of unqualified condemnation would stop such a force.

Around Maysville, Kentucky, Fee began to preach that "God hath made of one blood all nations of men." For a year he lived with his wife and child in a one-room cabin and farmed to support himself. Finally he erected, with modest help, a "free church of Christ" with no tyrants and no slaveholders. His church and the schoolhouse that he had built were burned. Two men who attacked him with clubs died soon thereafter.

The dedication of Mr. Fee, together with the intelligent challenge of his sermons and pamphlets, attracted the attention of Cassius Clay, a brother of Henry Clay. Through Clay's invitation, Mr. Fee became pastor of a church in Berea. This soon led to the establishment of Berea College, which has since become famous as a combination of sound education and character-building. The college owed much to his support in the troubled days before and after the Civil War.

There are similar hardships today as men strive for a Christian answer to the growth of cities and industry, the burden of world leadership for our nation, and prejudice between national and ethnic groups. A *Louisville Times* headline (June 18, 1964) announced: "Integration Views Oust 100 Ministers a Year."

The perils are continuous, even though the particular issue may change. From the apostle Paul we can learn some of the attitudes with which a Christian can face the consequences of prophetic action.

First, the apostle assumed that some affliction would be the lot of any aggressive Christian. He expected this for the new churches, and he warned them that he would suffer also (cf. 1 Thess. 3:1–4). In areas of the world where Christians are in the minority, such a statement is commonplace. It seems difficult to apply in areas where nominal Christianity is dominant, but one soon finds hardship when he deviates from the alliance of church with culture. Since most readers are in an area where nominal Christianity is dominant, you might ask: "What can I possibly do for Christ that would upset the world enough for trouble to ensue?"

In the second place, Paul admitted that persecution could crush him personally: "We were so utterly, unbearably crushed that we despaired of life itself" (2 Cor. 1:8). This should give pause to any "cultural Christian" who thinks that he is a prophet because he denounces petty sin. Would he be so vigorous in condemning the sins of a powerful person who could crush him economically or socially? And what about a man's family? A denominational worker in a predominantly Baptist state said: "People know where I stand and they talk to their kids. Now my kids come home crying because of what their playmates say about them. How much more of this can I let them take—especially when our schools are integrated this fall?" A man who remains proud in his strength has not suffered as a prophet.

Third, Paul did not talk about his suffering unless he saw that it would have some specific purpose for the good of others. When he wanted to correct the pride of those who had become satisfied, as at Corinth, he contrasted their well-being with his distress. This he did to admonish them, rather than to brag on himself (cf. 1 Cor. 4:8–14).

When it was necessary to distinguish between a true apostle and false apostles, Paul presented the endurance of a man's convictions under trial as a realistic test (cf. 2 Cor. 11:12–33).

If there were a need for others to become vividly aware of what it means to work for Christ, then Paul could show them what he had endured in order that he and others might obtain the grace of God (cf. 2 Cor. 6:1–10).

Fourth, Paul, who had endured so much, was not bitter about his suffering (cf. Phil. 1:3–18). So far as he could tell, it had helped to advance the gospel by drawing attention to the reason for his imprisonment. His hostility was not so much directed against those who persecuted him as it was against false brethren who undermine the church. Those who preached a gospel of works and self-afflicted martyrdom were the objects of his wrath (cf. Phil. 3:2).

Fifth, Paul did not rejoice in his persecution except for the sake of the church (cf. Col. 1:24–29).

Sixth, the result of suffering was to make Paul more humble. He exhorts others to find the same humility that Christ showed through his suffering (cf. Phil. 2:1–18). He says, "If I must boast, I will boast of . . . my weakness" (2 Cor. 11:30).

The Marks of a False Prophet

An immature Christian may blunder into a painful experience that seems like prophetic suffering to him, or he may take some impulsive action that seems to be zealous and dangerous. How can we tell that his is an ill-advised move? What is "false" about his motivation or judgment?

Diffuse indictment.—The speaker refers to "they," "those people in—," or another blurred label upon which the imagination of hearers may write the name of a personal enemy. When the words are finished, people may be angry, but each man is angry at his own enemy. The "prophet" has not specified his target nor told what he has suffered to bring his message.

Elusive participation.—The false prophet acts as though he is greatly concerned about many issues but adroitly glides away from those that really commit him. If he is asked, "What have you said to 'them' about this situation?" he may reply, "Well, they have not asked for my advice." Those who hate "them" will be satisfied, but a careful listener will know that the man has not answered the question. His personal responsibility is lacking.

Degrading references.—The immature prophet has nothing but scorn for those who disagree with him. He may be vindictive and sarcastic in attacking the motives of others whom he scarcely knows.

Martyr identification.—The false prophet is certain that he is the cause of a great commotion. There seems to be no recognition that some offense comes because of the cross of Christ and some because of our own stupidity and idiosyncrasies. The agitator does not realize his own limitations and has little humor with which to look at his mistakes. Instead, he identifies all reactions to him as a sign of his righteousness and identifies himself with Christ on the cross.

Personal aloofness.—The zealot seems to have no friends except those who share his drive for some particular object. There is no time in his life for friends, flowers, rest, or even for worship. He is too busy "doing the Lord's will" to rest in

the Lord, receive the comfort of the Christian community, or
wait to find out if he is really serving God or himself.

It would be excruciating for such a person to stop. He has
little capacity for conversation. Either he is silent, talking
about himself, or debating on some "great" theme.

The Vital Balance

The people whom I have just described are lonely and
isolated. They attack a hostile world that has—they think—
cheated them in some way. They solve their loneliness by
attacking the community. Dietrich Bonhoeffer issued an appropriate warning: "Let him who cannot be alone beware of
community . . . [and] let him who is not in community beware of being alone." [5]

A mature prophet is one who can be alone and like it.
Although he is sensitive to the needs of his age, he has taken
enough time for contemplation to know himself and his place
in this age. Personal communion with God has given him a
sense of eternal security that allows a certain nonchalance
about the honors of this world. This does not mean that he
claims to be immune to suffering but that he fears God so
much that he can thereby overcome his fear of men. Holy
awe burns out timidity.

Although the prophet speaks to the community, he is not
consumed by it. When rejected by his countrymen, he can be
alone at peace. He does not look for opportunities to cut off
relationships, but he can recognize with sadness that some of
this may happen.

There are some prophetic spirits that can bring originality
out of institutional religion. Jesus was an example to his disciples of one who brought voluntary religious service into

---

[5] *Life Together,* trans. John W. Doberstein (New York: Harper &
Bros., 1954), p. 77.

correspondence with an inner attitude of holiness. He presented them with a spirit of godly liberty in his discourses on fasting, ritual ablutions, and sabbath observance (cf. Matt. 9:14–17; 15:1–20; 12:1–14). All these things had been regularized and institutionalized by the Jewish nation. Jesus did not come to destroy the Law but to fulfil it. There were beneficent ends served by institutional religion which could be observed without falling into the petty scrupulosity of a cheerless legalism. In his analysis of *Jesus' Training of the Twelve*, A. B. Bruce observed that the best young disciples might be saved from unnecessary rebellion against arbitrary restriction and older disciples might be prevented from indulging in overconfident judgment on difficult points of religious details.

The old has not really passed away; it has just become new. With a new center for self the convert receives ancient truths with a creative impact. He looks for actions that will appropriately proclaim his new understanding of God's relation to man.

7
Joy and Suffering

The mystic is serene when he feels that he is completely in the presence of God, and the prophet is satisfied when he sees the will of God made real in the world. Both the presence of Christ in our lives and achievement in his name are sources of great joy.

The Joy of Salvation

The new spiritual sense of a Christian provides understanding of the duty and moral excellence of God's creation. As Jonathan Edwards put it, this is the joy of holy affections, a perception of the world and self that is full of glory.

Jesus taught that his disciples are to rejoice because their names are written in heaven (cf. Luke 10:17-20). They can enjoy this world and themselves because the basic problem of life is settled; they are at peace with their Creator.

Without this new center of holy affection, our feelings of joy are cut short. Our appreciation of God's creation is marred by predatory desires or guilty memories. We cannot look with childlike joy upon the essential beauty of this world. Man needs an innocent eye to know true loveliness.

The enjoyment of a gracious life is based on the joy of God in our salvation and our willingness to seek his guidance and forgiveness. The "fruit of the Spirit" is a blessed existence, which is to be as satisfying to the new believer as it is to those who witness to him.

When the virtues of a gracious life have become our nature, then we can handle the twin perils of praise and blame. Both of these can destroy pure joy. On the one hand, praise can lead us into unwarranted pride or undue abasement. These are snares to the soul, for they indicate that we do not know how to appreciate the approval of others for the true gifts of God in our redeemed life. Those who accept praise too readily need humility to take themselves less seriously. Those who cannot accept praise need confidence to know that others take seriously the contributions they make.

Joy can also be destroyed when we do not know how to receive blame. As we have seen in previous chapters, persons with an overdeveloped conscience can feel guilty about everything. They have not been taught to discriminate between their own responsibility and the responsibility of others. Although a mature person is sensitive to the general tragedies of life, he sees some difference between those for which he is specifically responsible and those for which he, as a human being, shares responsibility, though limited by his circumstances. There is no specific answer to the question: "Where does *my* responsibility end and *his* begin?" apart from an examination of specific cases.

The level of Christian growth can be seen in a person's reaction to criticism. An untried Christian, who is preoccupied with old faults and attitudes, is very vulnerable. A person in the midstage of Christian growth is likely to be less concerned. He assumes that his way of life is satisfying and that others should find the same for themselves. If someone points to his attitudes as the source of some social evil, he may shrug his shoulders or see that the church "votes out" an annoying preacher.

On a more mature level a Christian evaluates blame in the light of his previous experiences. If he has shared his life with other Christians, and they have helped him to evaluate his strengths and weaknesses, he will have poise as well as sensitivity in hearing the correction of others. He knows that a flaw in one area of his life is not the same as total failure. He has been redeemed and he lives in faithful relations with people who accept and forgive him, despite his limitations. This does not diminish his concern for his own and others' mistakes, but it gives him clear vision for evaluation and realistic knowledge of the resources that will remedy the situation.

This inner confidence may lead on occasions to a judgment against an accuser. For example, a mature Christian may accept some responsibility in the organizational life of his church and block out other periods of time for his family in the home or in recreation. If he is accused of a "lack of dedication," because the whole family is not at every church service, he might answer: "Your accusation assumes that my children are as old as yours. But they are not. The baby goes to sleep at seven every evening. So I attend evening services one Sunday and my wife attends the next."

The joy of conversion is about the only Christian satisfaction felt by some people. Although this is the primary source of blessedness, it is not the end. God has called us also to rejoice in his creation and be creative ourselves. God's creative activity is now to be channeled through the graciousness of our lives and the inspiration of our acts among men.

The Joy of Fellowship

Jesus was a new kind of religious leader. He spent more time at feasting than at fasting, more at weddings than at funerals. Luke's record of his life and spirit is filled with joy, from Mary's saying, "My spirit rejoices in God my Savior"

(1:47), to the disciples' return from the ascension "with great joy" (24:52).

Luke presented not only the teaching of Jesus about God's joy for those who found him (chap. 15) but also the living joy of Christ in the companionship of his apostles. He rejoiced at the success of their labors in his name (10:17) and that they shared with him in the fellowship meal that would precede his betrayal and crucifixion (22:15).

It was at that Last Supper that Jesus made his disciples the instrument of his joy in the will and love of his Father (cf. John 15).

Those who entered into the "joy of the Lord" were faithful servants. Their steadfastness was the source of godly approval (cf. Matt. 25:21). The staying power of a new affection is a sign of Christian maturity. It is built upon a new identity and satisfactions in a godly company.

We speak of this continuing identity as fidelity. It is sustained loyalty as a man of God. As Dr. Erik Erikson has said, this is a virtue built up in adolescence. Childlike trust is threatened by the contradictions of this world. The adolescent now has an opportunity to give up the value systems of his family and to cast his allegiance with other groups in society. Freed from the childhood struggle of becoming a person who may be held accountable for his actions, he now faces the question: "To whom do I wish to be accountable?"

When an adolescent pledges his loyalty to a group and that group confirms him as a member, from a human point of view his joy is then full. Personal commitment is now strengthened by confirmation. Liturgical churches use the word "confirmation" to express their approval and hope for a child's loyalty to God. Among Baptists and Disciples, baptism is the symbol by which the church acknowledges the conversion of a believer.

The joy of fellowship is, therefore, a sharing of personal

commitment among those who hold the same values and approve our exercise of them. This is the powerful combination by which a person meets the ambiguities of life. The gathering of believers is an individual's strength for the sufferings of this world. Jesus, knowing that he would face a cross, sat in joyous fellowship with his disciples. They had been with him in his trials, and though they would desert him for a time, their steadfastness would return in the strength of his resurrection.

Jesus knew the testing of loyalty in the persecution that would come upon his disciples. But he compared this to the travail of a woman who no longer remembers her anguish when a child is born. Those who suffer for righteousness sake will know sorrow in this world, but it will be turned into joy (cf. John 16:1-25).

The Meaning of Suffering

What does it mean to suffer for righteousness sake? And how is it possible for Christ and his disciples to speak of joy to those who are sensitive to the war, pestilence, national catastrophe, and personal anguish of this age?

There are several explanations of suffering in the Bible. The Old Testament makes no consistent distinction between physical and mental suffering. The writers of Psalms 6, 32, and 38 describe both the wasting away of the body and the sorrow one feels for sin. To the ancient Hebrew any kind of disease or misfortune was regarded as a symptom of personal sin. Joy left the soul at the thought that one had been brought near to "the pit" where sin, death, and hell combined. This primitive view of specific catastrophe as the result of individual sin was later challenged by Job.

The writings of the prophets sometimes present physical disaster because of sin, as when an entire city or nation might suffer. Amos promised the destruction of a heathen nation such as Moab. Israel was warned that drought and pestilence would follow a wilful transgression of the Law. At times national catastrophe might be considered a means of turning the hearts of people toward the Lord.

When Old Testament writers thought of the personal results of suffering, some of them found that it had taught them a specific truth. Through the agony of personal betrayal, Hosea learned what it meant for Israel to betray God.

The most thoughtful Old Testament passages on suffering are to be found in Isaiah. There, God is likened to a shepherd who will feed his flock (cf. 40:11). His servants will bear the sorrows and transgressions of men. Isaiah saw us as creatures whom God loves. God suffers with us to provide a means for our redemption.

The means of this redemption was dimly perceived in Isaiah as the Suffering Servant of the Lord. It was in the New Testament that the disciples saw what the prophets longed to see—Jesus the Son of God, the Suffering Servant, whose life, death, and resurrection brought redemption to mankind.

The cross of Christ is the distinctive contribution of the New Testament to the meaning of suffering. Jesus is the God Man, who both understands our weaknesses and triumphs over them. It is through his example while on earth and his Spirit living within that men can now triumph over human suffering (cf. Luke 22:42–44; 2 Cor. 4–5; Gal. 1:4; Heb. 4:14–16). The joy of the Christian is to have the spirit of humility that filled the obedient Son of God (cf. Phil. 2:1–11).

The New Testament gives a more complete understanding of the relationship between sin and suffering. Because some Old Testament passages spoke of suffering as a result of some specific sin, many first-century Jews concluded that all suffering could be traced back to the error of the individual who was afflicted. But Jesus specifically rejected this assumption. When the disciples asked whether a man who was born blind was being punished for his sins or his parents, Jesus answered, "It was not that this man sinned, or his parents, but that the works of God might be made manifest in him" (John 9:3).

In the Sermon on the Mount, Jesus said that the sun rises on the evil and the good and rain falls on the just and the unjust. In these and many other ways he taught that physical suffering was not necessarily the result of a specific sin.

The apostle Paul found that the buffetings and hardships of the Christian life had produced character in him when it had been accepted in a godly spirit (cf. Rom. 5:1–5; 1 Cor. 4:1–13). In this sense he could rejoice in his suffering, for it had been an occasion for him to understand the Word of God more fully and to proclaim Christ among men (cf. Col. 1:24–29).

The Burden and the Cross

We must use caution, however, when attributing creative qualities to suffering. There is some pain in suffering that is needless and inhuman.

Because suffering is such a complex and mysterious part of life, we must ask several questions, such as: Is this particular suffering necessary? Is it voluntary? For whom or for what shall we suffer? Is it necessary? For Christians at a very immature level it may seem that suffering is the justifiable result of a previous neglect of faith. Sometimes men can see a direct result between their careless way of life and the penalties which they suffer.

Persons with a vague sense of guilt sometimes tend to identify physical illness with God's punishment. For example, in a tumor and cancer hospital, many patients tell their chaplains: "I know why I am in here. It is because of the wrong things that I have done. Now I have this terrible disease." Cancer is looked upon as an unclean disease in the same way that tuberculosis was considered fifty years ago. Although many of these patients could not describe any specific attitudes or actions that were grossly sinful, they associated the presence of illness in their lives with their sense of guilt.

Behind this feeling was the assumption that God was marking up deeds and misdeeds and punishing or rewarding in this life. This view tells us more about the patient's mother and father than it does about God. Such a view is typical of an authoritarian conscience, which has been trained by reward and punishment without love and understanding.

On a more mature level, persons understand God as a just and loving Father, who does not remove the natural problems of this world from us, but who would teach us how to overcome them. With this encouraging view that comes from mature faith, Christians have challenged many forms of suffering that were thought to be "inevitable." Inhumanities to women and children, which were thought to be a "natural" part of certain cultures, have been curbed by Christians who believe that God would have them remove any stumbling block to those who are weak.

Much pain or trouble changes from "necessary" to "unnecessary" when the center of self is changed toward God. For example, in the First Church study, a wife told of the financial problems that came to her family because her husband was an impulse buyer. When he saw the new cars and learned that his brother-in-law had bought one, he could not resist the temptation to go into greater debt to keep up appearances. From his unregenerate point of view, this was "necessary" in order for him to hold up his head in the family. But a year after his conversion, his wife commented that he talked over purchases with her before he signed any easy payment plans. There was less conflict in the family because there was more trust and less debt.

A change of attitude is related to the second question about suffering: "Is it voluntary?" This is where the known and neurotic sense of guilt will differ. The person who suffers for a known cause can bear up because he has some purpose in life. Patients will move a limb under a medical therapist, despite great pain, because there is hope that this activity will lead to better functioning of the affected part. But in neurotic suffering the basic cause is not conscious. A physical illness of poorly defined origin may seem "inevitable" to a guilty person.

One doctor pointed out to a group of medical students that he had recently examined three persons with a common complaint. In each case the individuals responded well to treatment until they were tempted to commit the acts that had made them feel guilty in the first place. Each time they repeated their infidelity, their physical symptoms returned. When the physician sought to show the relationship between guilt and illness, his patients became indignant and placed the blame on him or some weakness in their body.

There are occasions when neurotic suffering may be more mental than physical. One man described how he "wore himself out" for his daughter's happiness. He "protected" her by taking her to all social affairs and driving her home. He spoke of this as a great drain on his physical strength. This would have commended him to responsible parents if his daughter had been thirteen or fourteen years of age, but people soon learned that his daughter was fully eighteen and most unappreciative of her father's "kindness." Although the man was very active in his church, a few people began to see that he was unwholesomely jealous of his daughter's boy friends.

On one occasion, the man went to a church at ten in the evening to see why his daughter had not returned from a young people's social. The director of youth activities met him at the door and assured him that he would see that the daughter was escorted home in a few minutes. The man replied, "There are no good young men in this community that I would trust to drive my daughter home." When the youth director and his wife offered to take the girl home, the father became furious and vowed that he would eradicate this "worldliness" from the church house.

As people talked over this explosive episode, they agreed that the father was overpossessive. He did not want anyone to take his place with his daughter, but he could not admit this. The suffering that came because of his jealousy was of his own devising. This man thought that he was "carrying a cross." But he had missed two of the distinctions between a cross and a burden.

The bearing of a cross is a conscious undertaking. It is an action or attitude directly related to Christian values. When a Christian experiences a trial for "righteousness sake" then he will be blessed (1 Peter 3:14). When the suffering is for the sake of Christ, we have a satisfactory answer to the third question: For whom shall we suffer? Joy is possible under these conditions when an individual finds that his normal resentments at the injustices he suffers are taken away. This is one sign that a person is working for something beyond himself. One nurse observed this when she worked for the Medical Committee for Human Rights in the deep South. The racially mixed teams of doctors and nurses offered medical advice to Negroes in areas where there were no outpatient clinics nor free drugs for the poor. Although she lived in a home that had been bombed and where the family was continually threatened by white people, she was surprised to hear no anger, hostility, or bitterness against white persons from her Negro host. She concluded, "This surprised me. I think there is a strong religious influence there." [1]

---

[1] *Washington Post*, August 18, 1964, A-26.

The Enemies of Abundant Living

The sin and suffering of this life are not sufficient in themselves to subdue a joyful existence. There are conditions, of course, under which people are perpetually depressed. In a nation-wide interview survey of 2,460 Americans, Gerald Gurin and associates found that the wives of poorly paid day laborers were really miserable. They had no economic security and little psychological hope. Their lives centered around material problems, for every day they fought for food and shelter. This is a challenge to mature Christians. Can we create the conditions under which such people will be free from these preoccupations?

About two thirds of the persons fortunate enough to live in America have a different preoccupation. Like most of the people who are able to buy this book, the middle-class American is more concerned about relationships with other people than he is about money for his next meal. Joy in life does not hinge so much on material possessions as it does on the people with whom we enjoy these things.

Dr. Gurin found that most Americans think of happiness or unhappiness in terms of financial *comfort* rather than in terms of *luxury*. He also indicated that a happy person is able to endure many temporary problems. In fact, a distinction could be made between a person's basic sense of gratification in life, which was happiness, and the way in which he invested himself in the lives of others, which brought him some worry. So, for example, mothers who *enjoy* parenthood still worry about the way in which they occasionally lose their tempers with their children. Fathers who enjoy parenthood have a different worry; they feel guilty because they are not with their children often enough or do not know how to feel close to them.

We may conclude that for some income groups, the enemy of joy is grinding poverty and no hope of job satisfaction or a happy home life. For other persons the chief problem is in the way a person relates to others. These are the channels of joy or sorrow.

How can persons continue to find satisfaction in their relationships when death, disease, and misfortune come? How can a Christian continue faithful service when he recognizes the entrenched evil in society and self? These questions bring us to the necessity of faith and the possibility of doubt, which are the subjects of the following chapter.

8
Faith and Doubt

Faith is confident reliance on God and enduring belief in the attainability of his purpose through our lives, in spite of the dark urges within us and the ravages and temptations of this world. It assumes a worshipful attitude toward an unseen God. Jesus presented the trustful expectancy and joy of a child in his presence as the spirit with which one would be received into the kingdom of God (cf. Mark 10:13–15).

A Godly Confidence

Faith begins in conversion. A right relationship with God is not to be sought in the recital of words nor the obeying of a system of laws but in him to whom we hold fast by believing. It is the faithfulness of our God that makes us righteous (cf. Rom. 1:17). Right living is a result of faith in the right person, even Jesus Christ our Lord.

Confidence in God's steadfast love is Christian. Belief that God will serve us like we want him to is popular religion. As we have already seen in the chapter on guilt and forgiveness, man can assume no easy relationship with his Maker. We are not to believe in God because he will bring to pass the events that we desire. Rather, we are to admit the fickle-ness of our goals and the faithlessness of our relationships and depend on a God who is constant in his loving forgiveness and just purposes for men.

For some converts religion is not faith but futility. These persons twist reliance upon God for their own convenience. With false assurance they assume that a profession of words, "Lord, Lord," will be reckoned as righteousness, despite their present nonchalance to God's will. How bitter will be the day when they find the kingdom closed against them (cf. Matt. 25).

Such "cheap grace" misses half the meaning of faith. The New Testament describes faith not only in terms of confident reliance upon God but also in terms of the hopeful attainment of his purposes through our lives. We are to pray for that which we are willing to see come to pass. If we have faith in God's forgiveness, we must also begin to take action by forgiving others (cf. Mark 11:22–25).

The attainment of God's purpose through our lives does not mean the perfection of all our ideals at one time. A previous chapter on the Christian conscience has indicated the deceptive nature of our conscience. That for which we hope may not be the goal that Christ has set for us.

A new Christian may not understand this and be continually cast down, because he fails to meet his expectations. He may need to be reminded that it is no sin to be human. We do not have all strength and foreknowledge. We will fail. Faith does not imply perfection as much as it demands trust in a God who will love, forgive, and lead us on.

Faith as the attainment of God's purposes may lead us through some of the sufferings that have been described in the previous chapter. In fact, people who have been broken by life may find that their willingness to suffer is the necessary component in their healing. This was the conclusion of Chaplain Melvin Kimble's study of mental hospital patients. He found that people who continually projected blame upon others or withdrew into fantasy as a protection against sensitive truths did not get better. Illness continued because they used these devices as a protection against those whom they thought would hurt them, or against self-knowledge that seemed too painful.

On the other hand, Chaplain Kimble found a healing force in the lives of those patients who were willing to stand the pain of self-realization. Sometimes they had to suffer through memories of early experiences that brought tears to their eyes. Or they might descend into the bleakness of despair, as they described the love that had been denied them and the defeats they had suffered in life. But out of this came hope for some that their suffering was not in vain. They had found a chaplain, doctor, nurse, psychiatric aide, fellow patient, or some member of their family who was helpful in their time of distress. Faith was no longer something prescribed for others; it was now a quality of life. They did not really know if they would be well or not, but they were willing to take the risk of pressing toward that goal.

The goal of Christian faith is life in Christ (cf. John 3:15, 18; 4:41–42). It is a gift of God, the result of God's drawing of men toward him (cf. John 6:44). For some persons this may be understood primarily as contemplation, as it seems to be in the Gospel of John. For others it will be a more active life, as expressed in the writings of the apostle Paul.

Whatever the expression may be, faith moves men to more mature living. There is a time when we cry out primarily for the relief of some stress, and on these occasions faith is the hallmark of healing (cf. Mark 5:34; 10:52). But Jesus calls men from a reliance on "signs and wonders" to a higher state in which there is joy in relation to him and commitment to his purposes, whether seen or unseen (cf. John 1:51; 3:12; 20:29–31).

There seem to be stages in the development of this kind of faith. First, God is faithful to us and draws us toward him. Then we experience faith as the relief of sins and as a source of new security for our lives. Finally, we think of our faith primarily as joy in the presence of an unseen Lord, who walks with us in a way of which we are not always sure.

Depression and Doubt

Faith is based upon faithful relationships, and a mature faith stands when relationships are unfaithful.

Christian faith is not based upon *our* assurance and confidence. Despair, depression, and doubt are common experiences in the lives of some believers. A faithful person is one who can cry out to God even in the midst of such distress: "Out of the depths I cry to thee, O Lord! Lord, hear my voice!" (Psalm 130:1–2).

Sin, misfortune, and sickness have their effect on a sensitive Christian. When a loved one dies, his spirits are very low. There may be a loss of appetite and restless sleep. These are common symptoms of depression that stem from obvious causes.

A sudden business reverse may sadden a jovial man. Worry and concern may oppress him. Any kind of separation from people may cause one to be more "moody" than usual. A move from the home community to a large city, or from one school to another may create loneliness and despair in a wife or in a child. The breakup of a romance may cause a young person to sit in a "blue spell" all day.

All these are exemplary reactions to severe loss or personal strain. In a healthy person, who has a background of reliable and loving relationships, these feelings are temporary. They are a testimony that he can respond sincerely to the tragedies and uncertainties of this life.

However, the moods of some people are unrelated to specific happenings. Their sense of depression comes from vague feelings of unspeakable guilt.

An example of this would be a wife who is always moody and irritable after a visit from her parents. She gets "boiling mad" when her mother rearranges the furniture and "takes over" the management of the children. The obvious favoritism of the grandmother for one grandson is a source of great conflict. It seems the daughter cannot openly tell her mother why she is angry. Instead, her indignation goes underground and she pretends that all is well.

On one occasion, when she did "boil over" in front of her mother, her husband took her aside and said, "You should be ashamed of yourself. Your parents are older and wiser, and a good deal richer, too. Let's get along with them."

This kind of unresolved resentment caused deep guilt in the young wife. Her hostility was turned in upon herself and her spirits were depressed.

When this young woman and her husband entered into a discussion group at a neighboring church, they were surprised to find people like themselves who, under the supervision of their pastor, talked about many of the same problems. One of these was the handling of hostility. Another was relationship to in-laws.

The young mother was too uncertain of herself to make any comment in the group, but she did ask for some time with the pastor. Out of these conferences she began to understand why she felt so depressed after a visit from her family. In time she gained enough self-respect to speak up to her mother without feeling guilty or impudent.

During this time, the pastor also requested some interviews with her husband and challenged him to be the head of his own house, rather than abdicating leadership to his aggressive mother-in-law during her visits.

Of course, there are times when solutions do not come so

quickly or happily. Sometimes the cause of depression is so deep and the reaction so severe that medical attention is required. It may be the tired, listless, apathetic feeling that results from some physical disturbance. Or it may be the result of childhood and adult deprivations that need extensive psychiatric attention. The person who sits in despair and says, "My life is not worth living and I am going to end it all," should be taken seriously.

Whatever the cause of depression may be, Christianity has a place for such feelings. Whether we ascend into a heaven of joy or descend into a hell of despair, our God is yet with us. John Bunyan presented this allegorically in many scenes in *The Pilgrim's Progress.* He began with the struggle of Christian and his companion Pliable as they had fallen into the slough of despondence. Pliable crawled out the way he had come in and this led back to the city of Destruction. But Christian waded on through the mire until he came out on the side near the cross.

Faith does not promise immunity from despair, but it does promise deliverance.

The Distress of Doubt

A faithful relationship to God also has a place for honest doubt. What Christian could be more puzzled than the apostles themselves? John records that the disciples were bewildered by Jesus' statement that one of them would betray him (cf. John 13:22). They did not believe him when he said he would rebuild the temple in three days. Only after the resurrection did they understand that this was a prophecy concerning himself (cf. John 2:22). Their confidence, as in the case of Simon Peter, sometimes gave way for sudden panic (cf. Matt. 14:31).

Jesus looked with compassion upon the struggles of Simon Peter to prove faithful and encouraged him. He gave Thomas specific evidence that his doubts might be dismissed. When he found the disciples startled and frightened after his resurrection he asked, "Why are you troubled, and why do questionings rise in your hearts?" (Luke 24:38). Then he gave them physical demonstration that he was, indeed, alive.

On some occasions our doubts are related to religious growth. For example, many young persons have questions as they make the shift from traditional loyalties of their parents to a personal loyalty to Christ. If a person is to make the Saviour personal in his own life then he must work out his own salvation with fear and trembling. In this process he may question many assumptions. He may discard the ways by which his elders express their faith.

The religious questions of adolescents often symbolize their rebellion against adults. On some occasions the young persons come through this period with a renewed appreciation for their elders. When older persons are considerate of the strivings of youngsters and pass on the hope that answers will come, then there may be a reconciliation between the generations. This is especially the case when adults indicate that they do not yet have all the answers and that they may have to learn some things from those who are younger, for they live in a changed world. At the same time, young people will respect older persons who have convictions that they have lived by with faith and a realistic appreciation of the changes that take place in our day.

Unfortunately, some rebellion is not resolved into renewed appreciation on both sides. A parent may be very domineering and require a young person to submit exactly to his views. As a result the youth may become cynical and disillusioned. He sees that religious beliefs are being used to make him conform. It is difficult for this young person to think of Christianity as a growing, courageous force in his own life.

In their flight from this kind of restriction, some young

persons reject both their parents and their parents' religion The God of our fathers is not necessarily identical to the God of our Lord Jesus Christ. But this distinction may not be clear to either parents or children.

The breakup of personal relationships is another common cause of religious doubt. This may take place because of the conflict of a domineering parent and an unyielding adolescent, or it may be some force that comes suddenly to shatter friendships. Death is one of these forces. One eight-year-old girl refused to pray anymore after she heard that her beloved grandmother had died. She doubted that God would answer her prayers anymore. When the mother was questioned about this she told her pastor: "Well, we have always tried to answer our girl's prayer in a literal manner. We would stand by the door and listen to the request that she made of God, then we would buy whatever she asked for and tell her that God had sent it."

Children recover from the grief of death when their parents are truthful and confident when talking to them about what has happened. At times the bereavement of the child is not over actual death but over separation, through moving away from a beloved playmate or the transfer from the fields of a farm to a crowded apartment in the city.

Among young people, broken courtships are a frequent temptation to doubt. This is especially true when the young person has listened to the teaching of popular religion, that there is "only one soul mate prepared for them by God." After prayer and a very idealistic courtship they may find that they are drifting apart, for reasons that are difficult for them to understand. Now they may think that their prayers are powerless and God is not giving them the destined one.

A mature Christian may be able to explain to these young persons that there is a good deal of trial and error in the process of courtship. The destruction of plans may be an opportunity for the young persons to learn something new about themselves. Their idealism may now come into new focus as they see some aspects of their lives that must be dealt with. A young man may have to admit that his jealousy did drive a young lady to despair, or a young lady may begin to see that she was expecting a perfect man, or at least one she could "make over" within a year or two.

The breakdown of relationships between parents and children may cause parents to question their own faith. A mother may begin to wonder how anyone who loves God could lose her temper so often with the children God has given to her. She may need the help of an understanding neighbor, Sunday school teacher, or pastor to see that the resentment against the children is caused by the excessive strain of twenty-four-hour duty, seven days a week. With no help from her traveling husband or distant relatives, the woman may turn against those who are closest to her during the day.

There are times when the shock of grief may induce a mature person to doubt God. "Why did God do this to me?" is a symptom of this problem. If a person has been taught that God "takes" people from us, then resentment builds. If I lost one of my children and a neighbor told me, "God wanted your child" I would certainly doubt the existence of that kind of God. The God I worship is neither cannibal nor arbitrary tyrant.

Persons of a prophetic spirit often fall into despair after long and lonely trials against community indifference. They may begin to doubt their own worthiness of or blame themselves for the suffering which others are bearing with them. Frontier Baptist and Methodist ministers were often prey to these feelings. Deprived of the natural attentions of their family and exhausted by their itinerant labors, they would become physically ill and begin to have doubts about the meaning of their ministry. For a period of several weeks

John Leland had "great distress of mind." He wondered how to address a congregation of sinners. He felt that his preaching was not right.

In our own day, men like Martin Luther King have described the emotional exhaustion and depressive doubts that fill a man who sees others suffer with him in a struggle that never seems to end.

On some occasions persons may have deep chronic doubts, which are too uncomfortable to mention. Such persons seek to control these feelings by protesting too much about their faith. Usually we can recognize these unhappy people by at least two characteristics. First, they loudly proclaim that they never doubt anything about themselves or the church. Second, they swiftly and viciously attack anyone who openly expresses any of the doubts already mentioned in this chapter.

9
Love and Judgment

Love is the final criterion of Christian character. It is the directing of God's sovereign will toward this world and its salvation; it is the active force in Christian men that demonstrates their calling by God (cf. Gal. 5:2 to 6:10 for one classic expression of this truth).

The Christian's perception and practice of love will be the measure of his growth in grace.

The first stage in grace is the removal of the inner conditions that have created barriers of hostility between man and God and between man and man (cf. Eph. 2). This isolation and guilt is broken down by the active love of God that establishes our identity as forgiven sons through Jesus Christ. This is the start of a good conscience. It must be molded and motivated by the Spirit of Christ, as he is revealed historically in the Scriptures and personally in the Christian community. Personal communion with God, the fellowship of his saints, and the instruction of the written Word supply good will to us and teach us how to show this same will of God toward others.

The converted person feels the impact of God's love for him and the love of other Christians for him. He is in a stage of receptivity as well as reorganization. In this condition he is much like a child who must receive loving-kindness before he can generate the same spirit from himself. Religious education has emphasized the years of affection and care by parents that provide fertile soil for a child's understanding of God. In similar fashion, pastoral care teaches us that a new convert, a babe in Christ, must be surrounded by the same tender feelings if he is to grow into mature manhood.

But Christian love is more than an attitude of receptivity. It is to have the quality of steadfastness that characterized God's love toward Israel. Hosea found that though the people had been as harlots, God would love them as a forgiving husband or father.

In the New Testament, those who love God are to be steady in their allegiance (cf. Eph. 3). Fickle and wayward behavior is condemned (cf. Gal. 5:4; Heb. 3:11–16). Growth in grace is a sign that God's love moves consistently through our lives (cf. Rom. 8:37).

Fidelity and steadfastness characterize the second stage of Christian love. They are similar to the human challenge of adolescence, when a young person seeks trustworthy objects of his affection and commits himself to those persons. For a fourteen-year-old boy, love is loyalty.

For the growing Christian, fidelity can be expressed in a concern for people, for institutions, and for ideas. Sometimes persons channel loyalty so much toward the church as an institution that they lose the sense of personal intimacy and creative idealism that characterize Christian love. It is necessary, therefore, for fidelity to be thought of as something more than blind loyalty, perfect attendance, or unquestioned acceptance of organizational structures.

Steadfast love should contain both the yearning of an adolescent for close friendship and his questioning and rebellious spirit. As we have seen in a previous chapter, the mystical spirit is one in which a person takes that which is an old truth and makes it new in his own life. Some questions have to be asked and some doubts raised before faith can really live in us. Faith received without question is conformity to the teaching of men.

When steadfastness has been added to the sustaining power of love the Christian has received, then he is ready for the exercise of grace—the third challenge of loving growth. Love at this level is reciprocal forgiveness in action. We have experienced the forgiveness in Christ, and now we seek to show that same spirit to others. As the conditions toward good will are created in us by the concern of Christians for our lives, so we may return this good will in our own attitudes and actions.

A gracious spirit is one that grows gentler under the correction of God, which forgives more easily as it sees more clearly the sin to be forgiven. It is steadfastness toward sin, because we know its power has been broken by Christ; and it is clear judgment toward others, because we have felt the result of approval and disapproval in our own lives. To be gracious, as our Lord was gracious, is to anticipate the hard places of life that others must face and help them to walk the way without stumbling.

This is the way of an adult. It requires a realism that lifts love above sentimentality and a steadfastness that carries it beyond an impulsive discharge of good feeling.

Finally, love becomes wisdom. The mature Christian not only senses the needs of others but recognizes his own power to help. His care for them may be a determinative influence in their lives. Love as wisdom combines personal sensitivity with self-limitation. In our culture, it will require slightly different orientations for men and women.

For men, wise love finds its primary function in risk and responsibility. Men are taught from boyhood to be aggressive. They are to provide for and protect women and children.

In some sections of every community there are men who are judged by this criterion alone. A woman will say, "Well, my husband is not home much and never looks after the kids, but he is a good *provider*." Or a boy will say, "My father never said much to me, but I know that he loved me because he always saw that I had the things I needed for school and college."

Christian love demands something more of a man than mere responsibility and the risk of going outside the home to make a living in the world. Christianity also requires that a man be sensitive to God and to those about him. It is not enough to provide bed and board for a family, a man must also give of himself if he is to be counted wise in love.

We sometimes see the wisdom of this by contrasting the lack of it. For example, studies of schizophrenic girls have indicated that their mothers were overprotective and their fathers were withdrawn. The father might be a "good provider," but he was so immersed in his business that he demonstrated few personal characteristics of a father around his daughter. Furthermore, he had retreated from his wife and the daughter sensed the lack of parental communication. Psychiatrists found that when the father could be brought back into the family picture, the girl would improve. When a father led a mother back toward himself, some of her inappropriate feelings were released from the daughter. When the father took a firm and realistic interest in his daughter, this was the care that aided her recovery.

In our society, a man must be more alert to the sensitive aspects of love than to the self-limiting factors. If he is active in this world's affairs, he will probably have enough frustrations to know the meaning of limitation. At least the opportunity for such learning is always there.

Our men are being continually reminded by theologians that the great sin is pride—an unwillingness to recognize the limitations of life. These limitations should be self-evident.

Most women do not need this reminder. The receptive nature of motherhood conditions a girl to look upon limitations as a part of femininity. Our culture supports this. A young lady makes herself attractive for marriage and waits in a suitable place for the man who is expected to propose. She may inspire him, but he will have to say something for himself. With marriage comes an additional example of receptivity both in sexuality and in childbirth.

As Valerie Goldstein [1] has pointed out, the temptation of the woman is to fall back upon culture and biology for an explanation of her being. A man is expected to prove his masculinity by strenuous activity or the development of talents, but a woman has indelible proofs of her femininity in the beginning of menses and the bearing and caring for children. By being receptive, things will happen to her that "prove" her place in life.

Mrs. Goldstein warns that passive acceptance of this receptive nature will mar the image of God in a woman. It will lead to an undeveloped and negative self, in which her talents as a person are too narrowly channeled. That is, she becomes so absorbed in mothering functions that she looses her capacity as an attractive wife and responsible matron in the community.

There are some tragic results when women become so sensitive about being a good mother that they abandon other opportunities for self-creativity. After World War II, the phrase "smother love" was coined to describe inadequate, indecisive young men who could not make the grade in military service. They were the products of the eroding anxiety of women who channeled all their affections into the

---

[1] "The Human Situation: A Feminine Viewpoint," *The Nature of Man,* ed. Simon Doniger (New York: Harper & Row, 1962).

protection of their "little boys." Such mothers had defined themselves completely in terms of their sons and could not bear to see the boy who was an incarnation of themselves become a man who would be himself.

The wise love of a woman is, therefore, centered more upon personality than it is upon reproduction. On a mature level, she has much more in common with her husband and brothers than she has in distinction from them. Biological differences diminish as the character of life between man and woman increases. In Christian faith there is a recognition that God has made male and female (cf. Matt. 19:4). This is the basis for the protectiveness of the man and the loving creativity of sexuality. But mature Christian faith also recognizes that in essentials there is neither male nor female in Christ Jesus. One goal of personal growth is required for us all, for in Christ Jesus we are all one (cf. Gal. 3:28).

Is Love Enough?

Mature love is founded on the acceptance of self by God. We then love ourselves and others because God has first loved us.

Because he has significance, a mature Christian does not try to use the love of others to increase his own selfhood. He is satisfied if they owe him nothing but to love him, and he in return will respect them for their individuality. Love has taught him in what ways he is like others and also those ways in which there are differences.

This self-security is essential for parents. It is so easy for a parent to try to extend himself through his child or to become vulnerable to the approval or disapproval of his child.

The parent who seeks to live his life through his child is creating an idolator. That is, he is setting up his own wants and desires as the ultimate source of being for his offspring. Such a person needs to be confronted with the New Testament commandment that children are to be brought up in the discipline and instruction of the Lord (cf. Eph. 6). The desires of the parent may be a channel of God's grace, but the vessel is not to be confused with the maker.

Although a youngster is not capable of acting on the basis of this separation until he is twelve or fourteen, he can at least be aware of the distinction at an earlier age. One five-year-old demonstrated this when her father was telling her good night. After she had prayed, she said, "Daddy, you are the best *earthly* father, but the Heavenly Father is God."

"How do you know the difference, Darling?"

"Well, Daddy, you make mistakes, but God never does."

The parent who can admit before his children that he makes some mistakes has reached a degree of maturity. Immature parents neither wish to recognize their own mistakes nor allow their children to make any. They are overpossessive and overindulgent. Without any self-security, such adults seek to gain security from the child by letting him "do just what he wants." The result is a child who begins to see the world only in the light of his own desires. He tends to view others solely in relation to what they can do for him. He "gets along" with people very well, so long as they conform to his requirements. He has never learned to weigh his wants against his ability to satisfy them.

Describing this condition, Peter Bertocci has stated that this type of self-gratification brings little self-satisfaction. There must be enough frustration in our lives for us to become sensitive to the needs of others.

Is it enough to be loved? Not if love means the self-indulgence that we have just described. Men learn the mature meaning of love through personal suffering, frustration, and sacrifice. We develop mature character out of a combination of acceptance and frustration that gives us both the strength and the control to stand in moments of stress. This is the basis of steadfast love; the ability to endure some struggle, to attain goals that bring lasting satisfaction.

When we have been accepted for love by our parents, yet taught the limits of our own desires so that we can love others, then we are lovable people. We know something of the rights of others and we can measure them against our own self-respect. We are able to invest ourselves in others because others have invested themselves in us.

Statements about frustration and judgment seem to go against the modern counsel to be "accepting," a term which is often undefined. Popular writers often seem to combine love with acceptance. But what is this acceptance? Upon what is it based? Often it becomes a vague substitute for specific standards of right and wrong.

Joseph Sittler, professor at the University of Chicago, has called this vague acceptance the "ethics of despair." Those who have lost all meaning in life have no judgments and no issues worth fighting for. They desire a comfortable life where nothing has any meaning. Everyone agrees to tolerate everything. This is the courtesy of nonsignificance.

Christianity has never promised this kind of acceptance. We are acceptable to God only under certain conditions. God judges us as sinners, incapable of saving ourselves. Therefore, he has sent his Son to save us. When we recognize ourselves as sinners and accept the reconciling power of Christ, then we are acceptable to God.

Does God's judgment of us as sinners take away his acceptance of us? No, the depth of God's judgment determines the depth of his acceptance. As the apostle Paul states in the book of Romans, the amazing fact is that the God who knows our blind sinfulness has shown such love for us that he sent his Son to die for sinners. It is not our love that has wrought acceptance, but his love for us under the most trying conditions.

If we were to think of this idea in terms of our own life we would see how relevant it is. We sometimes say, "Oh, he is a nice fellow," when we do not know a man well or do not wish to be bothered with him. Closer examination would mean more penetrating judgment; we might or might not be closer to the person as a result.

On one occasion a middle-aged woman sought out her pastor and said, "What do you think of people who have lived together for fifteen years and still cannot get along with each other?"

The pastor replied, "I would say that they had some deep problems that could not be easily solved. What do you think?"

The woman hesitated a moment and asked one more test question, "Surely this would not happen to good Christian people who pray and ask the Lord for help."

The pastor said, "Sometimes the problems are so big that we cannot find an answer by ourselves. This is why we need the understanding counsel of Christian friends."

With this, the woman sat down, sighed, and began a long story of marital difficulties with the words: "You won't believe what I am going to say, but. . . ." She was afraid that no one would accept her story. Hence, she had to ask questions to find out whether this pastor knew enough about human nature to listen all the way with understanding.

Can Love and Wrath Mix?

Since God knows human nature, does he love us or condemn us? The Bible tells us that he does both. How is this possible?

Since the Bible often describes the relationship of God in terms of parent-child, we might think of this relationship for an answer. God is not like a parent who will not interfere with his children because he might hinder their "self-expression." He is not an indulgent father who cannot bring himself to take stern measures, because he might inhibit his children or cause them to turn against him. As we have seen in the previous section, a mature father is able to take some risk and responsibility along with the development of sensitivity to the needs of wife and child.

The biblical writers picture God as a father who combines both responsibility with sensitivity. He is personally involved with the growth of his children. The Bible uses words like punish, chastise, wrath, anger, and indignation to express God's concern for the conduct of those whom he loves. These words are used to express the feelings of God because the biblical writers knew how much God cared for those whom he had created. The writer to the Hebrews put it this way: "The Lord disciplines him whom he loves" (Heb. 12:6).

Does this judgment come upon men because of the arbitrary wrath of God? No, it comes from our disobedience to God's gracious commands. As a result, men may feel and accept the salvation of God: "God sent the Son into the world, not to condemn the world, but that the world might be saved through him" (John 3:17).

God loves his children so much that he is willing to judge and forgive us. Judgment is one quality of his love. But at this point someone may draw back and say, "I cannot believe in a God who punishes people by killing them." This is a disturbing point, for there are Old Testament passages in which such divine vengeance is recorded.

These passages belong to the earliest history of Israel. In the later revelation of God to the prophets, he is seen as a God of steadfast and tender love, who judges his people and yet restrains his anger for a time in order that they may repent. In Isaiah God is pictured as a just and loving Father who suffers with his people for their sins.

In the New Testament Jesus speaks of both love and judgment. This was a change from the Old Testament pattern.

Although the disciples wanted to bring down fire on those who refused to receive them, the Lord would not allow it. God is still angry with those who disobey him, but the manner of punishment has changed. It is in the conscience of men and in the laws of nature that men now find the judgment of God upon them.

The final judgment of God was also proclaimed by Jesus. By referring to a final judgment, Jesus delivered his disciples from the Jewish error that every sickness or disaster was a sign of God's judgment for sin. When men told him of Galileans who had been murdered by Pilate, Jesus answered, "Do you think that these Galileans were worse sinners than all the other Galileans, because they suffered thus? I tell you, No; but unless you repent you will all likewise perish" (Luke 13:2–3).

If judgment is a part of love, how can it bring one back to God? Will it not drive men farther away from him?

Spiteful or easily changing judgment will cause men to reject God, but a steady and just punishment may bring relief from guilt and lead the sinner back to his Lord. James Dittes, psychologist at Yale University Divinity School, has affirmed that our feelings of guilt often persist and are not readily dissolved. They stubbornly resist mild reassurance or rebuke.

The sinner often needs some piercing experience of punishment by which the sin may be undone and swept away from him. Relief from guilt comes when we feel that the heart of the evil within us has been touched by purging punishment and forgiveness.

The judgment must come from God rather than men. As long as we are at the mercy of our own conscience, we are pitiful beings. But a just God can mete out to us the judgment we deserve. He is also the one who can bring forgiveness. We cannot forgive ourselves, but God can forgive us.

Hope for the Future

The completion of love and the finality of judgment will not be in this life. The frustration of love and justice is a part of our earthly human limitation. Although a godly conscience, a study of the Scriptures, and the counsel of Christian friends can aid us in knowledge of ourselves, there is a final judgment by God that shall bring to light the true purposes of the heart (cf. 1 Cor. 4:3-5).

The Christian looks to the consummation of his godly existence in the age to come, when the faith that sustains him now will become the basis for a more complete knowledge of himself and God. In the heavenly world we will be fully Christ's and we will know ourselves as he has known us.

Until that day, our purpose is to teach "every man in all wisdom, that we may present every man mature in Christ" (Col. 1:28).